The Parents' Practical Guide to

RESILIENCE

*for Preteens and Teenagers
on the Autism Spectrum*

by the same authors

The Parents' Practical Guide to Resilience for Children aged 2–10 on the Autism Spectrum
Jeanette Purkis and Emma Goodall
ISBN 978 1 78592 274 9
eISBN 978 1 78450 574 5

The Guide to Good Mental Health on the Autism Spectrum
Jeanette Purkis, Emma Goodall and Jane Nugent
Forewords by Wenn Lawson and Kirsty Dempster-Rivett
ISBN 978 1 84905 670 0
eISBN 978 1 78450 195 2

The Autism Spectrum Guide to Sexuality and Relationships
Understand Yourself and Make Choices that are Right for You
Emma Goodall
Forewords by Wenn Lawson and Jeanette Purkis
ISBN 978 1 84905 705 9
eISBN 978 1 78450 226 3

The Wonderful World of Work
A Workbook for Asperteens
Jeanette Purkis
ISBN 978 1 84905 499 7
eISBN 978 0 85700 923 4

Finding a Different Kind of Normal
Misadventures with Asperger Syndrome
Jeanette Purkis
ISBN 978 1 84310 416 2
eISBN 978 1 84642 469 4

of related interest

Parenting without Panic
A Pocket Support Group for Parents of Children and Teens on the Autism Spectrum (Asperger's Syndrome)
Brenda Dater
ISBN 978 1 84905 941 1
eISBN 978 0 85700 958 6

Helping Children with Complex Needs Bounce Back
Resilient Therapy™ for Parents and Professionals
Kim Aumann and Angie Hart
ISBN 978 1 84310 948 8
eISBN 978 1 84642 893 7

The Parents' Practical Guide to
RESILIENCE
for Preteens and Teenagers
on the Autism Spectrum

Jeanette Purkis and Emma Goodall

 Jessica Kingsley *Publishers*
London and Philadelphia

First published in 2018
by Jessica Kingsley Publishers
73 Collier Street
London N1 9BE, UK
and
400 Market Street, Suite 400
Philadelphia, PA 19106, USA

www.jkp.com

Library of Congress Cataloging in Publication Data
A CIP catalog record for this book is available from the Library of Congress

British Library Cataloguing in Publication Data
A CIP catalogue record for this book is available from the British Library

ISBN 978 1 78592 275 6
eISBN 978 1 78450 575 2

Printed and bound in the United States

CONTENTS

INTRODUCTION

This book came about because Emma Goodall, one of the authors, heard the following story from the other author, Jeanette Purkis, and thought about it, in that very autistic way of revisiting and revisiting the story over and over. Emma then phoned Jeanette and said, 'I think we should write a workbook for parents, to teach their autistic children and teens to be resilient.'

In 2012, I met a young man who had been diagnosed with Asperger syndrome when he was six years old, Adam.[1] He was 21 when I met him. I told Adam that I was autistic and had written a book and that I worked full-time for the Australian Public Service. He responded almost immediately with, 'That's not true.' In Adam's universe, being autistic and writing books and working full-time was impossible. I spoke with him for a while. Adam had left school when he was 15. In the ensuing six years, he had not reconnected with education in any form. It was evident that, as far as Adam was concerned, education and work were for other people. He had never ridden on the bus and didn't have a driving licence, so presumably he had been driven to every place he ever went to by parents or friends of the family. He had spent his six years out of school playing computer games in his bedroom. His only social connection was to family. I spoke to Adam's parents and could almost physically feel their anxiety for their son. They also didn't seem to think he was capable of much else other than playing computer games. They had been told how he was going to live a limited life due to his autism by a range of educators and clinicians, and this seemed to have become a self-fulfilling prophecy. Independence and resilience were missing in Adam's life. He seemed to have been done a great disservice by two things that are all too prevalent for autistic young people — an assumption by a large section of society that autism is limiting and that autistic people are less able to function in society, combined with the understandable anxiety

---

1   Names changed in stories throughout the book.

of parents who have been told throughout their child's life about all the challenges and deficits that come with autism and few or none of the positives. I really felt for Adam and wanted to address this issue somehow, for surely there were many more autistic young people in a similar situation. (Jeanette Purkis)

Adam's story is one of the many things that inspired this book, as it caught Emma's attention due to her passion for ensuring that other autistics are on a path to a good life. The story demonstrates the need for resilience in autistic young people. Resilience is essential for navigating the adult world and being a fulfilled person who can reach their potential. Both Emma and Jeanette can be seen as successful autistic adults, in that they both work and live in their own homes (with fur and human families). However, underneath that veneer, both women are still autistic and still struggle daily with sensory and communication differences in a non-autistic world. It is their resilience and drive to make a difference that enables them to learn from mistakes and move forward, even if that learning can take decades at times!

One of the challenges around an autism-spectrum diagnosis is that it can unintentionally lead to dependence and a lack of resilience and confidence in autistic children and young people, as is evident from Adam's story. The diagnosis – which should ideally be liberating and empower the autistic person to understand and value their unique experience of the world – can sometimes, sadly, result in dependence and disengagement. A focus on deficits and perceived incompetence and messages given to a child can result in autistic children and young people doubting themselves and being unable to take on challenges. Building independence and resilience is a great way to address this.

Several factors probably influenced Adam's challenges and lack of independence. Adam's story, however, is far from inevitable. Autistic children and young people have the capacity to be independent and resilient. The process of building resilience and independence in autistic young people can start at a very young age. The earlier the process of building resilience starts, the better. This book aims to empower parents of autistic children to help them promote resilience in their autistic preteens, teens and/or young adults. Independence can be taken to mean being able to live independently or requiring some support to live a fulfilling life. Being verbal is not a prerequisite for either of these, and many adults who do not use speech live happy and fulfilling lives.

If a parent thinks their child may be autistic, or even if they think they may not be, this book will be a useful tool for teaching resilience. All the activities are based on over 15 years of teaching and education consultancy experience and on autistic lived experience, and they have also been audited by a variety of different autistic adults and parents to ensure that the activities are beneficial.

This book is a practical, activity-based resource for parents of autistic children and young people aged between 11 and 20 years. The book provides parents with information on resilience and on the main developmental stages for autistic preteens, teens and young adults, aged from 11 to 20 years of age. The book is focused on guiding parents in supporting the acquisition of resilience and independence in their children.

The book will take you through life events and milestones at different ages and identify where difficulties and barriers to resilience may arise and how to address them. Discussion of each life event will include exercises that you can work through in order to more effectively build resilience and independence in your child. The information will help you understand what your child might be experiencing to enable you to better to assist them through their life journey.

This book is written from a strengths-based approach to autism and the view that autistic people interpret and engage with the world in a way that is different rather than deficient. Building resilience can set up autistic children and young people to navigate through life better and build their self-esteem and confidence. Resilience-building through childhood and teen years can have a significant impact on children's ability to successfully navigate life in adulthood and will help them to find their place in society and reach their potential as adults when the time comes.

The book will take you through what resilience is, why it is needed, and what the risk factors and protective factors are around resilience in preteens, teens and young adults on the autism spectrum, as well as the challenges they may face. It will work through a number of life events that preteens, teens and young adults generally experience, including going through puberty.

Discussion of each life event will include helpful information and activities to enable you to guide your child through the event successfully and build their strength and confidence. The book will include information on how to ascertain where the child is in terms of their resilience. There are also activities around a number of life events experienced by teens and young adults in the spectrum, including starting high school, exploring sexuality, coping with the death of a relative or a pet, teenage parties, decisions around alcohol and other drugs, relationships and dating, making decisions around further study, and learning to drive. The book includes performance indicators showing what a good outcome at each life stage might look like for your child. There is also a chapter on failing successfully. Being able to manage failure is an essential life skill for everyone, and particularly for autistic kids who may be anxious around failure and mistakes.

Meltdowns and shutdowns are mentioned throughout this book. An autistic meltdown or shutdown occurs when an autistic person is overloaded, whether with emotions, social input, sensory stimuli, anxiety or other overwhelming experiences. A shutdown is an internalising response to being overwhelmed and a meltdown is an externalising response. Both of these are unintentional behaviours, and are almost impossible to control. Autistic people do not have meltdowns intentionally, and they generally feel very bad that a meltdown has occurred.

A meltdown is an indicator of overload rather than poor behaviour. Building resilience and confidence in an ever-increasing range of environments and activities can help to minimise the frequency of autistic meltdowns. Over time, many autistics develop the ability to cope with new or challenging situations, with resultant meltdowns happening later when the autistic is in a safe place, such as at home after school or work. However, without resilience and confidence, even adults struggle to manage their meltdowns.

Punishing or fixating on meltdowns is unlikely to help your child address their challenges and may, in fact, be counterproductive. If your child is experiencing fewer meltdowns, this is an indication that they are managing life events better. This is a very positive indicator of their ability to manage in the long term.

CHAPTER 1

RESILIENCE AND AUTISTIC PRETEENS, TEENAGERS AND YOUNG ADULTS

WHAT IS RESILIENCE?

When used to describe people, 'resilience' is defined as: *the ability to recover readily from illness, depression, adversity, or the like; buoyancy.*[2] Resilience is essentially the capacity to 'bounce back' fairly quickly after a difficulty or an adverse experience. Resilience basically involves working through any challenges or difficulties encountered in a proactive manner that will enable you to build confidence and mastery in overcoming that difficulty. Through doing this, a person can build mastery and confidence in other areas of their life, without even realising that they are doing so.

People who do not often have to face adversity or overcome challenges do not have the opportunities to develop resilience and are more likely to struggle in the long term even with minor difficulties. In contrast, people who have experienced and overcome a range of difficulties in childhood will have developed resilience as they have grown up. This means that parents, families and educators all have roles to play in helping children and young people experience, manage and overcome difficulties in ways that naturally scaffold the development of resilience.

Resilient people tend to be more able to face and overcome challenges and disappointment with positive outcomes in terms of personal growth and mental health. They tend to be more confident and willing to take on new activities and challenges and less anxious about change. The act of overcoming or managing a difficulty often gives people the confidence and skills to take on and overcome further challenges in life. Resilience impacts on a person's sense of self-worth and self-esteem. It is

---

2   Source: http://www.dictionary.com/browse/resilience (accessed 5 December 2017).

a key skill for living and is an important protective factor for mental health and well-being.

Resilience is in a sense a self-replicating skill. For example, once a young person has resiliently managed a challenging situation, they will most likely be more confident about their ability to overcome other challenges that they might encounter. This means that having resilience facilitates confidence, skills and attitudes, which feed into a person's ability to take on challenges, which in turn can mean that those challenges are less traumatic. This means people are more confident about their capacity to take on difficulties and less worried about their ability to deal with whatever challenges the future might hold. This in turn gives the person confidence and their ability to be resilient increases.

Resilience is a key life skill for everyone, including, or perhaps especially, autistic people. This book is written from the insider or lived-experience perspectives of the autism spectrum by two adults who have had very different but equally successful resilience journeys. In other words, both authors have built up enough resilience that they are able to manage the challenges that they face in life, both big and little, in ways that enable them to live as successful autistics who are, for the most part, comfortable in themselves.

This book aims to impart information that will enable parents, educators and other caregivers to facilitate the development of resilience in all the key areas that autistic preteens, teens and young adults need in order to successfully set up these children and young people for meeting the challenge of their adolescence.

WHAT IMPEDES RESILIENCE?

A number of factors can make it difficult to acquire resilience. These include:

- *Invalidation.* 'Invalidation' refers to situations where a person's identity, self, safety, experience or beliefs are invalidated by others. Invalidating experiences can include bullying, abuse, violence, discrimination, 'gaslighting' or bigotry and vilification. At its simplest, invalidation is the statement 'You can't', whereas a validating statement that could be used instead would be 'You are learning how to', or 'I am learning how to teach you' or, at the very least, 'You can't yet.' Autistic children, young people and adults often experience invalidation. Invalidation impacts on self-image and self-esteem. Acquiring resilience requires a degree of self-confidence and positive self-esteem, which invalidation strips away from a person, leaving them less able to take on this skill.

- *An assumption of incompetence.* Assumptions of incompetence are often directed at autistic people. These can take a variety of forms and include the idea that autistic people are not able to make decisions on their own behalf, to live independently, to work, to have friendships or relationships, or to raise children, and a great many other assumptions. For autistic children this can mean that their capacity to learn, to play, to communicate and to interact socially is questioned and dismissed. Assuming incompetence is in effect both invalidating and disabling a person. A simple example would be getting to school on the bus. If someone is not given the opportunity to get the bus to school, they may be assumed to be incapable of doing so, and therefore they will not learn to do so. In this way, people may begin to think that their assumption of incompetence was correct, and it can thus become a negative and damaging self-fulfilling prophecy that disables children and young people.

- *Issues with self-identity and belonging.* Autistic teens and young people often have difficulties 'owning' their own identity. This may result from invalidation by others or simply from the young person picking up on negative messaging around autism – and, by association, themselves. This can lead to them 'acting' like those around them in various social groups in order to be accepted. This acting is essentially them believing that they cannot be accepted for who they are, and thinking that their character or personality is deficient. It is hard to build resilience when you feel that you cannot be yourself.

- *Paternalism/shielding from difficulties.* This is a less obvious issue, but one that also hinders the development of resilience and can prevent people from achieving their potential. In some instances, people who are caring for someone may have low expectations of that person's capacity to do things that others take for granted. This attitude, of shielding people from challenges or difficulties, can be seen in parents and carers trying to protect their children from short-term or long-term pain or hardship. Many autistic people, and autistic children and young people especially, have experienced this. However, even if the child or young person feels loved and protected as a result, paternalism can lead to the child or young person losing confidence in their own capacity to do things. Self-doubt impedes the capacity to be resilient.

• *Negative messaging about who you are.* Negative messaging is a part of invalidation and gaslighting but also a key aspect of prejudice. Messaging about who you are impacts on your sense of self in relation to others. For example: a New Zealander is seen differently in New Zealand to Australia, where the messaging about what it means to be a New Zealander is quite different from 'back home'. Many autistic people go through their lives being told only negative things about themselves and about autism in general – not only by bullies but also in some instances by carers, educators and other professionals, and sometimes even by their parents. A young person who has only been told what they *can't* do often internalises those messages and this leads to difficulty in acquiring resilience. Autism being perceived only in terms of deficits rather than strengths can compound this, just as a young person internalising racist attitudes would perceive their ethnicity differently to a child who internalised more positive messages about their heritage.

• *Previous failure.* This can be both a learning tool and/or an impediment to developing resilience. A history of failing at an activity, particularly when the mistake is emphasised and focused on by adult role models or important peers, can have a negative impact on resilience. The failure can become a traumatic memory, making it almost impossible for the young person to try that activity again. This can be compounded by negative responses to the failure that denigrate the young person instead of putting the failure into perspective and encouraging them to move on. This experience can be compounded by 'failures' in several areas of life being emphasised and focused on, which often results in the young person avoiding taking on any new challenges at all. In the same way that overcoming one challenge can promote ongoing resilience in different areas of life, this kind of trauma relating to failure can result in effects that flow on to other activities, making the person less likely to attempt not only the activity at which they failed but also other activities. However, if the failure is used as a non-judgmental discussion point[3] to evaluate possible future responses to a similar situation, it can *support* the development of resilience.

- *Perfectionism.* Perfectionism often results in a high level of anxiety and fear of failure around a specific activity as the young person seeks to complete the activity perfectly. Perfectionism can result in a fear of failing. It can also occur in someone who feels they lack control in their life, who may feel a need to control what they are doing and to ensure that it is 'perfect'. Perfectionism can actually prevent a person from attempting the activity in the first place, due to their anxiety that they will be unable to do the activity well enough – or, if they do start, it can impede them from completing what they are doing in case it isn't 'good enough'. Perfectionism makes it very hard to build resilience and can often be mistaken for work avoidance or bad behaviour, for example when a young person fails to hand in schoolwork because it isn't 'right' yet or when they do not start work because they are worrying that it may be too hard to complete it perfectly.

WHY DO AUTISTIC PEOPLE NEED RESILIENCE?

While resilience is a valuable skill for everybody, autistic people, and children and young people in particular, have a great need to acquire resilience in order to achieve their personal potential and to maximise their well-being. First, autistic people face specific challenges that may set them back in terms of confidence and self-worth. They may find navigating the largely non-autistic world frightening, anxiety-provoking and invalidating. Autistic people of all ages may struggle to communicate their needs. Some may be non-verbal for part or all of the time and, while communication methods and devices are available, not all autistic people who need these have access to them. Even autistic people who speak can

---

3   References to 'conversation' and 'discussion' in this book refer to communication in the most effective way. This may or may not involve verbal speech, and includes such means as Augmented and Alternative Communication (AAC), typing, video, etc.

struggle to understand and explain their needs, especially when stressed. Change or a lack of predictability can be overwhelming. With some autistic children and young people, the very idea of doing new things can induce anxiety, meltdowns and shutdowns. Given these considerations, the attribute of resilience, which allows a person to be more confident in the face of adversity and change, is particularly important to acquire.

Without resilience, children and young people can go through life finding things increasingly challenging and becoming more and more anxious about taking on new activities. They may become autistic adults who cannot engage with society, leading to wasted potential for that person and the wider world. Their anxiety will increase exponentially, decreasing their quality of life. With the development of resilience, however, although anxiety may not cease entirely, it will rise and fall with lower and less frequent peaks.

Instilling resilience in autistic people, while best started early, can be supported at any age. The journey to resilience is a long-term one, and resilience can grow and develop continually through life.

HOW CAN RESILIENCE CHANGE YOUR CHILD'S LIFE FOR THE BETTER?

Resilience is helpful for autistic children and young people in a number of ways, including these:

- helping them to navigate life's milestones in a positive manner that promotes growth and knowledge

- building their self-confidence and self-esteem

- enabling them to build a strong, positive self-identity

- helping them to manage change and/or unpredictability

- helping them to recover from setbacks and disappointments

- helping to reduce stress, overload, and meltdown and shutdown

- helping them to succeed in challenges, and also to accept and learn from mistakes or failures

- helping them to understand the need for practice and patience when developing a new skill

- helping them to develop assertiveness

- helping them to set and respect reasonable social/emotional boundaries

- laying the foundations for life as an independent adult, whether they require a lot of assistance or only a little in that life

- assisting in their social interactions with difficult peers

- fostering a genuine sense of place in the world ('belonging' in the widest sense of the word), and thereby removing the need for acceptance by any peer group in order to feel they belong

- building their confidence in taking on challenges

- providing them with a solid base from which to move forward into adulthood.

HOW DOES A PERSON ACQUIRE RESILIENCE?

Resilience is a skill that is essentially acquired through experience. Practice really does make perfect when building resilience and independence skills. Every skill which a child or young person acquires can be seen in terms of them building their skills incrementally. For autistic children and young people, these skills may sometimes take longer to develop and may require a greater degree of support from parents and educators. If autistic children and young people are adequately prepared for a new life experience, they are more likely to pass through it with confidence and proficiency, and it will be less likely to be traumatic.

In this way, mastery of one experience or life stage is likely to flow on to other events or skills. Embedding resilience skills, when started young, can scaffold that person's development. This is likely to result in a greater degree of confidence in adulthood.

For anybody, the key to building resilience is to face challenges and difficulties and to overcome them. Of course, some things that potentially build resilience might instead result in trauma and heightened anxiety or other mental health difficulties. No parent would want their child exposed to that. The key to building resilience with children and young people – including those on the autism spectrum – is to introduce a series of controlled challenges to help them incrementally take on slightly larger challenges and build their resilience. It is not a good idea to expose anyone to failure upon failure, which would have the opposite effect!

Setting out to develop resilience is like setting out to run a marathon. Although you could just get up one day and run a marathon, that would be the most risky and problematic way to approach the goal. Instead, most people would increase their fitness and stamina over time by running short distances and gradually increasing the time and distance they run as they felt more confident and successful.

It can help to view resilience as a muscle that can be developed and grown through the 'exercise' of taking on new challenges. As the young person masters one challenge, they will ideally build their strength to take on the next. For this to be effective and supportive, there are a few considerations to take into account, and these will be covered later in this book.

Parents – and particularly parents of children on the autism spectrum – are often very reluctant to expose their child to difficulty in any way, shape or form. They may not want to expose their child to the possibility of failure or disappointment, and are often highly protective. While noble and understandable, autistic people – and all people – experience challenges, setbacks and failings throughout their life. For an autistic child who is likely to be acutely sensitive around failure or setbacks, building resilience through dealing with challenges can be a very good thing. If you imagine, for example, that a child is shielded from difficulty until they move out of home at the age of 20: how much more will a setback or error impact upon them then than if they had been supported in acquiring resilience at an earlier age, starting off with small, controlled challenges introduced by supportive parents and/or carers? There are a number of points in this process that parents may find hard to navigate. One of the aims of this book is to better equip parents with the knowledge of when and how to introduce challenges in their child's life – challenges that are supportive and effectively build resilience.

It may be helpful for parents and carers to understand that many autistic adults ascribe their ability to manage as well as they do in life to being resilient, and that having had parents who expected them to manage and to overcome challenges from early childhood was key to that resilience. Autistic adults who struggle more with life and who are less resilient have often experienced lives that did not support the development of resilience, but were instead invalidating and assumed long-term incompetence.

WHAT DOES RESILIENCE LOOK LIKE FOR TEENS AND PRETEENS ON THE AUTISM SPECTRUM?

There are some things that help you to see the growth of resilience in autistic preteens, teens and young adults. These include things like their being better able to identify and articulate their needs and wants. They may also be more able to decline an activity that is harmful, such as when peers bully them by asking them to do things that would make them look foolish or might result in injury. It's said that resilience is linked to self-esteem and a sense of self-worth.

Resilient preteens, teens and young adults may also be better able to set and to understand boundaries. This is another valuable skill which can promote self-worth and scaffold emerging assertiveness and self-confidence.

Resilient autistic preteens, teens and young adults may feel empowered to take reasonable steps toward independence. In this regard, it is important to note that some autistic preteens and teens want to leave home or take on other adult activities when they are not yet at a point where this is likely to be successful. While it is important to support a move to independence, it is also important to know when to apply the brakes. On the other hand, some autistic young adults make the transition to independence at a young age quite successfully. Where this transition involves quite drastic changes, such as moving across the world independently, it is often successful because the young person is following a long-term passion or interest.

KEY CONCEPTS AROUND RESILIENCE

The key concepts that should be taught to autistic preteens and teens include:

- Self-confidence – e.g. 'You are valuable just as you are.'

- Self-protection – e.g. 'You do not have to agree to do something with your body or actions just because someone says you should – even a friend.'

- Failing successfully (this will be covered in more detail later in the book).

- Perseverance and staying power – the idea that they may need to keep trying in order to succeed.

- How to make use of helpful criticism and to disregard negative criticism, and how to know the difference.

The 'place of safety'

The concept of a 'place of safety' relates to a home (or school) environment in which an autistic child is supported and encouraged. The place of safety is a key component in building resilience, as it gives a solid basis for the child's or young person's levels of self-esteem and self-confidence – both attributes that are strong foundation skills for building resilience. A place of safety does not mean that the child or young person is not challenged when required, nor does it mean there are no consequences for them. The place of safety is an environment of love and trust which forms a starting point for growth. A place of safety does not stop when the child turns 18 or when they leave home – it is an ongoing support throughout childhood and adulthood. As a child grows to adulthood, they can internalise the place of safety and take it with them, even if they are not physically living at home.

Ideally, a child will be supported within a place of safety from birth all the way through to their adult life. Just like other teens, autistic teens and young adults may want more independence and may challenge parental views. This can look as though they are not consciously aware of their place of safety or as though they are disrespectful. This can be a difficult time for everyone involved. Parents may be angered by their teenager's comments and actions. It is easy to stay with the anger, but this is rarely useful. In a place of safety, assertiveness and clearly defined boundaries and limits, rather than anger and aggression, are used by parents. While parents aren't saints, it is important to try to stay calm and to set boundaries for your teen, rather than yelling and dishing out unhelpful punishments devised in the heat of the moment. While it can be hard to remain calm and assertive, doing so will be of great benefit to your child and their notion of trust. In addition, consistent and clear rules and consequences are important for autistic preteens and teens, who can become very distressed by inconsistency of rules and consequences.

Building self-esteem

Self-esteem and self-confidence are essential building blocks for resilience. In the preteen, teen and young adult years, concepts of self-esteem and self-worth are being developed and tested. Invalidation, including things like bullying, exclusion and disrespect, can take a huge toll on self-esteem, and this will impact on the ability of the young person to acquire resilience. Conversely, validation, love and support can create an environment that fosters self-esteem and through that resilience.

What does self-esteem look like?

For autistic young people, self-esteem may look a little different from self-esteem in their typically developing peers. Given the challenges that many autistic young people face, what a parent needs to know about supporting and promoting their self-esteem may be different from the approach adopted by parents of typically developing young people.

Some actions parents can take to boost self-esteem include:

- making sure their preteens and teens feel included in the family

- validating and supporting their preteens and teens – being 'in their corner', especially in difficult times

- emphasising their preteens' and teens' strengths and skills, and not focusing on errors and deficits

- loving them in a way that makes sense to them – if they do not enjoy hugs, for example, demonstrate your love in other ways with which they *are* comfortable

- celebrating their achievements

- respecting and understanding teens' need for greater independence and their growing desire for privacy

- maintaining their sense of a place of safety throughout their childhood and teen years and as they grow to adulthood

- setting boundaries and limits that support them in staying safe and making more positive choices

- taking an interest in their interests.

Self-esteem looks slightly different at each life stage. Between the ages of 11 and 20, there are many changes happening, such as puberty and adolescence, a growing wish for independence, and a greater sense of individual identity.

Qualities demonstrating a growing sense of self-esteem in children aged 11–14 include the following.

- They speak about themselves positively.

- They have some ability to challenge people who are disrespecting or invalidating them (including through speaking to a parent or teacher).

- They approach the world in an increasingly enthusiastic or positive way.

- Imaginative play and fantasy world play is defined through characters who are positive or supportive.

- Passionate interests are mostly focused on something positive, not 'dark' or disturbing.

- Friendships are with children who respect and support them, not with children who belittle them or encourage them to do damaging things.

In teens and young adults aged 15–20, self-esteem might be demonstrated by the individual in these ways.

- They view themselves positively (most of the time or increasingly).

- Their activities and interests are not, or decreasingly, self-destructive.

- They are future-focused and able to discuss what they might do after finishing school, such as further study or work.

- They are positive, or increasingly positive, about the future.

- They can take on board some constructive criticism about themselves and use it to build resilience and understanding.

- The friends and/or partners they choose are respectful of them.

PROTECTIVE FACTORS FOR RESILIENCE

Specific protective factors that will assist your child in developing resilience include the following.

The capacity to communicate effectively

One of the key differences between autistic and allistic[4] children and young people is that they communicate differently. This can result in misunderstandings between these groups, and this in turn can lead to bullying behaviour or result in autistic children and young people being socially isolated and excluded. Communication is not a one-way thing, so it can be helpful to build the autism literacy of allistic peers and adults who interact with autistic children and young people (including teachers, clinicians, etc.). The difference in communication does not make one or other style 'correct' – both are valid: it's just that the autistic communication style is in the minority and historically has often been considered problematic or 'not as good'.

For children and young people who are non-verbal, it is essential to encourage them to communicate in whatever way works for them. The goal with a non-speaking child is not to get them to speak but rather to be able to communicate effectively. Effective communication is thankfully not limited to verbal speech. Whatever method of communication works for the child or young person, use that. Being able to communicate their wants and needs, as well as their thoughts and views, is essential to anybody's ability to build their resilience.

School/further education/work environment

Having a supportive environment where they spend their day is a key protective factor – be that at school, in further education or at work. Positive education and work environments include qualities such as peers and managers, teachers or lecturers not being bullies but instead supporting and validating the teen or young person. In fact, at school, in further education and at work, the positive social interactions and characters of peers and managers can be seen as a key protective factor around resilience. Feeling able to ask questions or seek confirmation and to feel that the people they interact with are kind and positive is a great protective factor for taking on new challenges and building resilience.

A school or workplace may have a positive and inclusive culture or a negative, toxic one. The nature of the organisational culture impacts on

---

4   Allistic is a term used in the autistic community as a descriptor for people who are not on the autism spectrum and not neurodivergent in any other way.

almost everyone there, but negative cultures will have a greater impact on people with lower levels of resilience. A toxic school or workplace is not only unpleasant but for an autistic young person can colour their entire experience of school, further education or work, and can therefore impact negatively on their resilience and confidence in similar settings and/or situations. Cultural change is difficult, and in some instances it will be preferable to leave the situation, particularly if it is impacting on the young person's mental health in a significant way.

Opportunities to take on challenges

Being given the opportunity to take on reasonable challenges and difficulties is at the very heart of resilience. These opportunities can sometimes be easier to provide with younger children because parents can control a lot of the variables. Some young people might want to take on challenges, while others might be more reluctant.

This is one of those 'Use your judgement' moments. You know your own child. Trust yourself and trust your instincts. You will probably know whether it is good to promote more independence or less. Know that you cannot protect your child from every little issue, and that in fact it would be counterproductive to do so. The older children get, the larger the consequences of their mistakes tend to be, so it is understandable that parents are concerned. However, the experience of taking on new challenges is an essential part of building your child's resilience.

This book includes a lot of information that will help you to support your preteen, teen or young adult through this process.

Supportive friends and parents

Having friends and family members who are genuinely supportive and who encourage positive choices is a strong protective factor for developing resilience and independence. It is very helpful if friends and family members set and respect reasonable boundaries and set a positive example for preteens, teens and young adults. In addition, family members and friends can assist the young person in taking on new challenges and can support them through the process, thereby directly supporting the development of resilience in autistic teens and young adults.

Supportive service providers and clinicians

Service providers, including health practitioners and mental health clinicians, can support autistic teens and young people in many ways in building their resilience and growing independence, including:

- addressing underlying anxiety and other mental health difficulties which might impact on the development of resilience

- supporting the autistic preteen, teen or young adult in taking more responsibility for their own health and well-being, such as through physical exercise

- challenging them to move a little bit beyond their comfort zone and support them through the process

- supporting them in focusing on achieving their goals and can assist this process by helping them to develop an effective strategy.

In the same way that helpful services and clinicians can support and promote independence and resilience in autistic preteens, teens or young adults, services and clinicians who are unhelpful, blaming or ableist, or who come from a strong base of viewing autism only in terms of deficits, can threaten the development of resilience.

CHALLENGES TO RESILIENCE

There are several issues that impact on acquiring resilience for 11- to 15-year-olds.

Being invalidated

Invalidation takes different forms, and the sorts of invalidation someone experiences may vary according to age. For example, unemployment is not likely to negatively impact a teenager (unless it impacts their family more broadly). Autistic children and young teens tend to experience invalidation related to school or family dynamics, including bullying, violence and abuse. Other invalidations can be less direct: things such as their family having a low socio-economic status or the breakdown of their parental relationship can be experienced as invalidating.

Moving into the teenage years can involve invalidations unlike those experienced in childhood. Homophobic or transphobic bullying, fat-shaming, being excluded from peer groups and falling behind academically are some of the new kinds of invalidations that teens can face. Although the particular invalidations may be new, the impact of invalidation on acquiring resilience and independence is similar: it is damaging and needs to be addressed. However, understanding the specific source of invalidation and/or its impact can assist you in addressing your child's needs around building their resilience.

Being denied the opportunity to take on challenges

As discussed earlier in the book, being denied the opportunity to take on challenges is something that can be seen as producing a self-fulfilling prophecy.

Imagine that an autistic teenager wants to learn to drive. Her parents and teachers do not think she will be capable of driving. When she wants to take the driver education course at school, she is actively discouraged. She asks her parents and teachers to help her get her licence, but each time they tell her 'No' and explain all of the reasons why they think she shouldn't drive. As a result, she never has the chance to find out whether she would have been able to drive. When she is a young adult and doesn't drive, people think this is because she can't and was never able to. In fact, she might have been able to drive or she might not have been – as she never had the chance to try, she will never know.

One of the authors of this book can and does drive. However, she struggled to learn to drive initially and, like many other teenagers, she failed her first driving test. Over time and with extra lessons she was able to pass her test and now drives daily, both long and short drives. The other author has never driven. For some autistics, the driving instructor's ability to communicate clearly and calmly is vital; without this, they may struggle to learn to drive with confidence.

These sorts of situations come up a lot with both schools and employers and families as well. Autistic people are often considered incapable of doing something. Sometimes they are seen as being unable to do the thing; at other times the thing is seen as being too risky for them to attempt. This may be for a variety of reasons, including personal safety or concerns that they will fail and that this might impact negatively on their sense of self-worth. In fact, denying autistic people the chance to try new things represents an approach counter to that advocated in this book: using controlled challenges and allowing exposure to the possibility of learning from setbacks and 'failure'. Shielding autistic young people from the possibility of failure, especially if this continues over a long period of time, is *not* shielding them from difficulty. Instead it may well be setting them up for a life limited by perfectionism, fear of failing and under-confidence.

Expectations that are too high

The opposite of denying autistic young people and teens the chance to take on new challenges is giving them too much to do or having overly high expectations of them. When autistic people are aware of an expectation or given a challenge, they often develop a strong focus on achieving that goal. Expectations that are too high can be as much of a curse as expectations that are too low, with the teen or young person wanting to live up to the expectation but terrified that they will 'fail'.

This is often overlaid with unhelpful labels such as 'high functioning' or 'low functioning' – a problematic concept which seems to doom those considered 'low functioning' to few or no expectations and to place unrealistic expectations on the 'high functioning' people. Those deemed 'high functioning' may not receive assistance if outwardly they are coping when in fact they are really struggling.

Mental health difficulties

Mental health issues and illnesses often manifest during the teenage and adolescent years. Autistic people have a significant risk of mental ill health, particularly conditions such as depression and anxiety disorders. Trauma, bulling and invalidation can impact significantly on the mental health of autistic young people. Many autistic people have alexithymia ('emotion blindness'). This does not mean that they lack emotions but rather that they struggle to recognise and describe what they are feeling. When young people have alexithymia, conditions such as depression or anxiety can go unnoticed by parent/s and teachers, and may also go unnoticed by the young person themselves. This can result in delays in accessing assistance and can compound the mental health issues.

It is difficult to build resilience when depressed, and incredibly hard to take on challenges of any description when experiencing mental health issues. Some of the messages autistic young people get from friends may also compound mental health issues. For example, many teens – autistic and non-autistic alike – engage in self-injurious behaviour. Peer-group pressure or bullying, or even alexithymia, can result in autistic teens engaging in self-harm in order to feel or to be accepted by peers or in an attempt to fend off further bullying. Mental illness and mental health issues pose a significant risk factor to resilience.

Being denied agency in decisions

Many people shield autistic children and young people from difficulties, concerned that the stress of taking on a new challenge or failure at something could result damaging them in some way. Autistic young people can go through life largely being denied any agency or choice in what they do in case it results in failure, anxiety or meltdowns. Yet as children grow through teenage years to early adulthood, they need to be given some opportunity to have responsibility for decisions that affect them. If they are not, they will likely become adults who do not know how to take a decision or how to be responsible for what they do.

This denial of agency in decisions that affect them can be a high-risk factor around acquiring resilience. It is almost impossible to build ongoing resilience if you never have the chance to take a decision for yourself.

Having no boundaries

The opposite of having no say in your own life occurs when parents give in to their child all the time. Many parents of autistic children fall into this trap if they become concerned that no other parenting strategy will prevent or minimise distress, stress or meltdowns in their child. However, this parenting strategy is often disastrous for autistic children, for a variety of reasons:

- First, the autistic child develops no concept of boundaries and will usually then resist the imposition of anyone else's rules or ideas, which creates enormous problems at school. In addition, in the long term this makes it almost impossible to hold down a job in which the autistic person is working for someone else.

- Second, as they are never challenged, the autistic child will not be able to develop any resilience.

- Third, the autistic child will not be able to develop their potential, as their family does not challenge them to learn any new skills.

The impact of having poor boundaries

An example of having no boundaries is when a parent allows a child to do anything they want to do. This can result in the young person controlling the family TV, for example, and refusing to let anyone else choose what is watched. In addition, the family may well be required to eat only specific foods, and to ensure that at every meal the young person has the specific plate, cutlery and glass that they see as theirs. Some families have to stop having other people over to visit or going out as a family. Other consequences of having no boundaries for the child can be that the mother or father is required to spend over an hour each night settling the young person into bed.

Sadly, restrictions on family activities will increase as the young person without boundaries gets older. Other consequences may be exclusion from school, which may follow incidents in which the young person has refused to do anything they were asked to do, because at home they are used to getting their own way all the time.

AUTISM AND THE 'TWO PUBERTIES'

Many autistic teens experience puberty differently from their non-autistic peers. Typically, parents expect their teens to go through the *biological* aspects of puberty, such as growing breasts, at the same time as going through *social/emotional* puberty, such as showing an interest in sexual intimacy. However, these tend not to occur together for autistic young people, who often experience emotional puberty a number of years after biological puberty.

Because of this, the social differences between autistic teens and their peers can *increase* rather than decrease. This can be very hard for some autistics to come to terms with, unless they have developed some resilience around social interactions. Many autistic preteens manage better in school prior to puberty than they do during the time when their peers are going through puberty. Biological puberty changes the basis for social interactions for most young people, and the consequences for autistics of this not occurring at the same time as emotional puberty are huge.

For example, young people experiencing both biological and emotional puberty can be focused on a new social hierarchy of 'desirable' friends and potential sexual partners, whereas an autistic young person who has not yet started emotional puberty can be left behind socially, bewildered by the changes in peers they have known for many years. Explicit information about these changes is really important for autistic young people: they need to understand what is happening in their peers and to be aware of certain risks so that they can minimise other people's ability to exploit them sexually or socially.

> I started my periods in my first year of high school. I was devastated because I thought that it meant I couldn't go swimming as the blood would leak out into the pool. After my mum had sorted that out by explaining about the difference between tampons and sanitary towels/pads, I had new struggles. All my friends and classmates seemed to go through some mysterious change and were all talking about sex and who they were or wanted to have sex with. The year before we were talking about music and TV and then bam. It was so strange. I joined a church youth group, and even there it was all about sex and who was 'going out with' who, even if no-one actually went anywhere. There was lots of alcohol available at youth group, and even though I didn't like the taste, I would drink it to try and fit in and belong to the group.
>
> Many years later, one of the girls from youth group said they could tell how drunk I was according to whether or not I would smoke the weed that they offered me. I had no recollection of this at all, which I guess indicates I drank far too much. Now, as an adult, I know these people were not really my friends, but at the time I thought that they were. I would advise parents to talk openly and honestly with their teens about alcohol, drugs, sex and how to know if people are really your friends or not. I think I was just a source of fun and amusement for the people at youth group. This still makes me sad. (Lil)
>
> I heard Tony Attwood talk about girls and women on the spectrum and adolescence, and he said that there are two kinds of autistic girls, those who are good girls and those who have lots of sex, take drugs and drink. It occurs to me, that probably applies to all teens, it is just that parents of autistic girls think that their children will never belong to the second group and so it is unexpected! Autistic boys often struggle because their parents don't expect them to date or have sex and so don't tell them

all those key unwritten rules that would help them know the difference between persistence and stalking, for example. (John)

The impact on resilience of teenage 'attitude'

Autistic teens are similar to all teens in some respects. The preteen and teenage years often revolve around different activities and new life choices. This is true for autistic young people across all cognitive abilities and among those who speak or are non-speaking. The push for greater autonomy and challenging parental attitudes, whilst it can be difficult or frustrating for parents, is actually a very healthy part of a young person building their sense of self.

Autistic preteens' and teens' attitudes can result in a number of behaviours, such as these:

- *Challenging parental structures and authority.* This can manifest in a variety of ways, some of which can be concerning or upsetting for parents.

- *Finding a different way of viewing their autism diagnosis.* This can mean either that they embrace their autistic identity or that they try to hide their autism to avoid being left out or being obviously different from peers with whom they would like to gain a sense of belonging. They may take on or create new elements to their persona which they think will make them more likeable to non-autistic peers. This can include things that do not have a huge impact on their well-being, like speaking in a different accent, taking on new interests, or changing the way they do things so that they appear more acceptable to non-autistic peers and friends. However, they may also start to do things to fit in with a peer group that can severely damage their well-being, such as taking drugs, vomiting after eating, or engaging in unprotected sex.

- *Becoming rebellious.* Some autistic preteens and teens may become rebellious, whether against their parents or society more broadly. Unpleasant though this may be for parents, as long as it does not put them in danger, rebellion can be a positive sign that young people are building an identity for themselves.

Identity, self-esteem and resilience

The preteen and teen years are an incredibly important time for the development of a person: their identity and their sense of who they are. This is particularly true for autistic teens and preteens. Autistic young people tend to receive a lot of negative messaging about who they are, both from bullies and more broadly from peers and adults who may have little understanding of the impact of their words and actions. The 'deficits' thinking and negative messaging can take a huge toll on an autistic young person; their sense of who they are can become damaged, and such messages can limit their expectations for life outcomes. Some autistic young people even seek out negative experiences, believing that they deserve to be unhappy. The best counter to this negativity is for parents, educators and other important people in their child's life to scaffold a positive identity. This scaffolding can come from seeing autism as a positive attribute and feeling good about identifying as autistic. Having autistic role models or mentors can be a great way to support a positive self-identification.

Supporting positive views of autism, and more broadly of neuro-diversity, can come as a challenge to parents, many of whom will have experienced clinicians focusing on their child's possible deficits and will also have had a number of negative interactions with the school administration if their child has done or said something inappropriate at school. Despite the useful traits that are part of autism, such as the ability to hyper-focus and to see details, the world tends not to view autism as anything other than a deficit. Many parents of autistic children challenge that entirely deficits-focused view and see their child's strengths and unique value, which is great.

Autistic identity

A positive autistic self-identity can include a number of elements. Generally, some attributes of a child or young adult who has a positive sense of who they are will include:

- not being ashamed or embarrassed about their autism

- feeling affronted when somebody puts them down (rather than turning this inwards into self-hate or insecurity)

- being able and willing to talk/communicate about autism with peers and adults

- engaging in imaginative play – or, for older children and teens, creating stories and written work – that includes elements of autism and/or autistic characters

- being willing to watch movies and programmes and to read articles about autistic people.

THE VALUE OF AN AUTISTIC/ NEURODIVERGENT PEER GROUP

For autistic preteens and teens, as well as for autistic adults, being connected with peers who share similar experiences and thinking is highly beneficial as it can help to foster a deep sense of belonging, of there being others in the world who are similar to them. Autistic children often gravitate towards neurodivergent peers without any prompting. This is understandable, and can be likened to being in a foreign country and finding people who speak your language.

Not having to think about everything you say in case the person you are talking to misinterprets it certainly makes friendship easier. Autistic people also tend to operate openly and honestly, and when speaking with autistic friends and peers there is little worry about misunderstanding words or ulterior motives behind interactions. Having peers who 'get' you can be a great protective factor around building resilience.

> When I heard someone talking about their experiences of being on the autism spectrum, I was so happy – finally I had found someone who might understand me. I talked to them after and we really did understand each other. Even though we have really different interests, we take delight in some of the same things and the way that we think is similar too. I spent so much of my childhood feeling different and alien: now I don't, which is nice. (Cara)

CONTROLLED CHALLENGES AND SUPPORTED RISKS

Building and establishing a sense of resilience and independence can be seen to come from the young person undertaking a set of controlled challenges – incrementally more challenging activities that build their strength and confidence, enabling them to get through difficulties and build resilience. Controlled challenges work for children, teens and adults, and are effective with autistic and non-autistic people alike. The basis for acquiring resilience starts with these controlled challenges.

> Jenna is 13. She lives at home with her mum and their dog Buster who is 11. Jenna loves Buster. When she gets home from school, she always gives him pats and cuddles. Over the past 12 months Jenna's mum has given Jenna a little more responsibility around looking after Buster. In addition to pats, Jenna now feeds Buster, brushes him once a week and gives him his heart worm tablet. Jenna and her mum have discussed the value of adding responsibility and how it will help Jenna to be responsible in other areas.
>
> Last week Jenna took Buster for a walk for the first time. She was a bit concerned as she hadn't done it before. Her mum was with her, and when they went home, Jenna felt really proud of herself and like she had achieved something. Jenna is going to ask her mum about whether it would be a good idea for her to take Buster for a walk by herself one day. (Jenna)
>
> Rick wanted to have a new computer game, but his mum said he had to buy it himself. Rick was 14 and did not have a job, but his mum encouraged him to think of ways he could earn money. Rick sold some of his old toys and computer games on Trade Me and found out about how to exchange old games for other second-hand games. It took Rick longer than he wanted to buy the new game, but after a couple of months he could see why his mum wouldn't just buy him new games. He even started breeding and selling fish on eBay to make more money when he wanted to buy an expensive game that was coming out. (Rick)

Controlled challenges can help your autistic child, teen or young adult to be more willing to take on new things and to manage change. In the introduction to this book, we introduced Adam, a child who had been shielded from difficulties throughout childhood. The impact this had had on him was twofold – he was extremely anxious around anything going wrong, and he was unable to do the things which most other young adults can do, such as studying, employment and living independently. Of course, as a parent you need to get the balance right: you don't want the challenge to become traumatic or to increase stress levels to a point where the exercise backfires and your child ends up more anxious about the challenge than before.

It is important to note that the capacity to take on new challenges will depend on a number of factors and will be different each day. As the parent, you will be the best judge of how your child is progressing with each controlled challenge. You will need to observe their response to the challenge and how they feel about it. You do not need to adhere strictly to a schedule around controlled challenges. There is no harm in postponing or cancelling a particular challenge if it is too much and may be harmful rather than beneficial.

Preteens, teens and young adults can be involved in building their own resilience too. Resilience can be a goal or project to work towards. Depending on your child and how they approach life, you may be able to talk about taking on challenges with them and setting targets. Be aware that your child may not always feel happy about being challenged!

The relationships between younger children and their parents is different from the relationship between preteens/teens/young adults and their parents. This is true for those with all levels of cognitive abilities, and for those who speak as well as those who are non-verbal. When a child is young, the relationship with their parent is more like that of a staff member with a manager: the 'manager' (parent) sets the rules and limits and enforces them. As children get older and go through the teen and young adult years, however, this tends to change, although it is often not clear cut at what point that change occurs. Autistic children particularly need guidance as they are developing independence. It is important to understand that young adults and adults can have high support needs and still develop independence. Independence in this context does not necessarily mean living independently without any support: rather it means being in control of aspects of your life, such as what you eat, when you go to sleep and what you wear. You may well need to transition from being your child's 'manager' to being their mentor, support person and critical friend. Building resilience is a journey you and your child can make together.

CHAPTER 2

RESILIENCE AND AUTISTIC CHILDREN AGED 11–15 YEARS

COMMON CHARACTERISTICS OF AUTISTIC CHILDREN AGED 11–15 YEARS

Autistic children between the ages of 11 and 15 years face a number of transitions and new experiences, including starting secondary or high school, biological puberty, and changes in the social expectations of themselves and their peers. This is a critical stage in development, which can strongly influence their journey to adulthood and their level of resilience.

Children and young teens may experience a lot of negativity in relation either to their autism or to their personality, or both. Sadly, this damaging messaging doesn't just come from school bullies – it can also come from well-meaning educators, friends of the family, siblings, or even their parents. Conversely, positive messaging can be effective in supporting older children and young teens and in helping them to view themselves with confidence and to build their capacity to acquire resilience. The messaging you give a child or teen on the autistic spectrum may have a significant impact on their thinking and self-perception, though you may not be aware of this. Given how crucial self-esteem is in supporting the development of resilience, it can be helpful to consider what messaging your child is getting, and to address any negative views where you can.

GETTING A DIAGNOSIS IN PRETEEN OR EARLY TEENAGE YEARS

While many autistic children get their diagnosis in early childhood, many others get it later. This can be particularly true for girls, who may miss out on a diagnosis when they are younger due to the more limited understanding of clinicians in relation to the presentation of autism in females. Due to a limited understanding of female autism in wider society, parents may also not realise that their daughter might be autistic.

With young children, it may be easier for parents to talk about the child's autism and to explain what it means. A younger child may have no memory of life before they got the diagnosis and may see it as part of themselves, much in the way that they have brown hair or like potato chips. When someone is diagnosed in late childhood or as a teenager, however, there can be some issues around assimilating a diagnosis if they have previously heard a lot of negative things about autism generally. This can lead to a difficulty in accepting, or even a refusal to accept, a diagnosis. Often this difficulty in accepting the diagnosis comes from a place where the young person doesn't like or accept themselves. They may form the view that autism is 'uncool' or that it justifies them in being socially isolated or in experiencing bullying.

Some autistic preteens and teens accept their diagnosis and consider it just as part and parcel of their identity. They may have friends already diagnosed, or, if they have felt 'different' for some time, the diagnosis may validate that view and give them a community to identify with. Each person is different in how they view their diagnosis. Parents need to be aware that issues around identity and belonging may be brought up by the diagnosis. An autism-spectrum diagnosis can be a big thing to take on board and to assimilate into their understanding of themselves and their place in the world. It is important not to view the diagnosis as something that should be kept secret, as doing so can often be interpreted as meaning that the diagnosis is shameful in some way. Not telling your child about their diagnosis is also unhelpful. Older children and teens will probably be aware that they are being assessed for autism, so it might not be an option to keep the result from them, but in any case it is always best to tell them. Recall old movies you may have seen in which a child discovered they were adopted by finding their adoption papers. Some autistic people experience this in regard to their autism-spectrum diagnosis, and it is an experience best avoided. Autism really is nothing to be ashamed of, and sending the message that it is a shameful thing will impact on your child's ability to value and respect themselves as an autistic person, which in turn will have an impact on their ability to build resilience.

Some older children or teens might ask for a diagnosis themselves because they know about friends or siblings who have been diagnosed or have seen information about autism online.

I am 32 and on the autism spectrum. My younger brother got
an Asperger's diagnosis when he was ten. I was older and could
see a bunch of the same characteristics my brother had in myself.
I asked my parents to send me for an assessment many times, but
they never did. I think they thought I didn't need a diagnosis
because I was doing well at school, but for me it was about
more than getting help. It was about understanding who I am.
As soon as I got a job and could afford to do so, I went and got
an assessment and found out I am on the autism spectrum. It is
great that I got an official diagnosis. I am now active in the autism
community and feel a strong sense of belonging there. (Kerrie)

AUTISTIC CHARACTERISTICS AND RESILIENCE

There are a number of attributes that autistic people often, but not always,
share. Many of these continue through life. They include:

- a strong connection to passionate ('special') interests

- a different style of communication

- difficulties in understanding non-verbal communication

- heightened and/or muted sensory experiences

- naivety in trusting others

- attention to detail and focus

- honesty

- a logical approach to problems

- feelings of isolation or loneliness

- a divergent thinking style

- hyper-empathy, which may be expressed atypically

- difficulties in executive functioning

- atypical interoception (the sensation of what is happening within
  the body, such as the sensation of temperature, pain, hunger or
  satiety, and the awareness of emotions)

- 'black and white' or rigid thinking

- a greater likelihood of gender divergence and of non-heterosexual sexuality

- an honest use of language, communicating exactly what they mean and meaning exactly what is being communicated – it is highly unusual for autistics to be manipulative, although people often assume this is the case

- susceptibility to certain mental illnesses or related conditions, including depression and anxiety disorders

- facing higher levels of bullying, abuse or other invalidation.

WHAT ARE RISK FACTORS FOR RESILIENCE?

There are some experiences relevant to autistic preteens and teens that can impact significantly on their life and that can be seen as significant risk factors which may impede the development of resilience. These include the following.

General risk factors

Anxiety

For many autistic young people, anxiety is a constant companion. As children grow older and as schoolwork becomes more complex, as do relationships with their peers, anxiety can become more pronounced.

Anxiety is often present when autistic young people do not know what to expect in a situation. For young children, things like social stories or role plays provide a good way to support them as they experience a new situation. Older children and teens do not always respond as well to these kinds of prompts, often thinking them juvenile, so it is important to find some other way of conveying what a new situation might look like in a way that is meaningful to the young person. There is good evidence that video self-modelling can be an effective strategy for children and adults of all ages.

As children get older, it can be harder for them to predict what is likely to happen in a new situation. If you say that a situation is going to look like X, and in fact it looks like Z, this may damage the trust between you and your child. It is important to be aware of the changing levels of complexity of social and other situations in the preteen and teen years.

These differences can make the world an overwhelming place, and this can impact on the development of resilience. It is much better to give a range of possible outcomes rather than just one that may not occur.

The weight of expectation

Expectations placed on autistic young people can sometimes create a barrier to resilience. Low expectations are often based on the belief that the young person is less capable than they are. This is a particular problem for autistic young people who do not (yet) speak, as they are often assumed to be far less capable than they really are. In this case the young person may not be offered the opportunities to do things that other people perceive as being too difficult for them. This is disabling in itself, and also promotes a belief that there is no point in trying.

On the other hand, expectations that are too high can be just as invalidating for autistic young people: they may begin to feel like failures if they can never reach the targets set for them, or if they can reach those targets only at the cost of their mental health because they spend so much time, effort and mental energy trying to live up to unrealistic expectations placed on them of which they are all too aware. This is most common where autistic children are average or above-average in some skills but struggle in other areas.

Perfectionism

While perfectionism might sound like a good thing, in fact it tends to be problematic: it can result in autistic preteens and teens being unable to engage in any activities for fear of failing or of not living up to the extremely high expectations to which they hold themselves. Perfectionism is a significant barrier to resilience for many autistic young people. It is almost impossible to take on a new challenge if the young person is terrified of failing and feels that they need to get it 100 per cent 'right'. In a school setting, behaviours that occur as a result of perfectionism can also be misinterpreted as the person being incompetent and unable to do the task or even deliberately refusing to do schoolwork.

Being shielded from all difficulties

Being shielded from difficulties is a subtler barrier to resilience, but its impact can be severe. If perfectionism is caused by the young person fearing failure, then shielding them from difficulty is the parental equivalent. Shielding autistic young people from difficulty may happen where parents are concerned the task might be too challenging for their child, that it might result in trauma, or that they will be unable to do it, which may lead to the parent thinking 'Why put them through it in the first place?'

A young person who is shielded from all difficulty may become unwilling to take on new challenges or unable to build their resilience. While the shielding is most likely done with the child's best interests at heart, it may have the opposite effect to the one intended. If a person never gets the chance to do something challenging, it is almost impossible for them to build resilience and independence.

Specific risk factors
Social anxiety

Starting at high school is a major transition for autistic preteens. It will involve meeting a lot of new students and teachers, as well as being in an unfamiliar environment, with unfamiliar patterns of moving around between lessons. This can pose significant challenges for autistic preteens and usually results in a lot of social anxiety. The nature of socialising also changes in the move to being a teenager, and autistic children can feel left behind as conversation with peers moves from things like *My Little Pony* or *Minecraft* to how attractive a certain classmate is or what jeans to buy.

Issues around belonging

Autistic preteens and teens may or may not feel pressured to fit in at school and other social settings, but in either case they may find themselves unpopular and ignored or ostracised. Many autistic young people, and particularly girls, will adopt new behaviours or attributes in a bid to be accepted by their peers. Often this can appear to be chameleon-like as they copy particular peers when around them. Another term for this is 'masking'.

Issues around identity

Difficulties with identity can result from this 'acting like their peers' to try and fit into a peer group.

Changing behaviour and attitudes in order to fit in can come at the cost of a young person's identity and/or their well-being. While it is easier not to be bullied or excluded at school by looking more 'ordinary', the nature of 'acting' differently in order to be accepted by others can result in autistic young people having to do a lot of work to understand who they are when they get older. Acting can be viewed in some cases as a kind of self-invalidation, whereby the young person sends themselves the message that they should change their character, as it is undesirable and unlikeable to be who they naturally are. This can be detrimental to a number of positive attributes, including self-esteem and resilience.

Puberty

Puberty can be confusing for all those going through it, but for autistic children and teens it can be very confusing indeed. For young men, having erections and wet dreams can cause concern. The unpredictable nature of their body doing unexpected things and possibly resulting in embarrassment at school can be very challenging. For young women, periods and growing breasts can likewise be a cause for concern. Many autistic girls have issues with periods for a number of reasons – the potential for embarrassment at school; concerns around hygiene; and their own heightened sensory perception means that girls may be anxious that others can smell with the same degree of acuity that they can. Some girls cannot tolerate tampons, whilst others struggle with sanitary pads/towels. It is important to discuss the sensory issues of both, as well as the practical issues of changing and disposing of sanitary products. For young people who are trans or gender-diverse puberty can be particularly traumatic, especially if the young person is not allowed to live as the gender with which they identify. This can in fact be quite dangerous and can result in suicidal and self-destructive thoughts. Information about puberty provided to autistic teens needs to be very clear so that it is not misunderstood.

Awkwardness and embarrassment

Awkwardness and embarrassment may be generalised or related to a number of experiences, particularly at school. Many autistic adults recall an embarrassing moment from over 20 years ago, despite the fact that it is unlikely anyone other than them remembers it! This fear of embarrassment can stop autistic preteens and teens from understanding activities or trying new things. The best counters to a fear of embarrassment are self-confidence and resilience. In addition, preteens and teens who can manage an embarrassing moment and move on from it confidently will be more able to feel comfortable in themselves and around others.

THINKING ABOUT SEXUALITY

Recent research suggests that autistic people have significantly higher rates of gender divergence and non-heterosexual sexuality. This is true of young people and adults alike. Homophobia and transphobic bullying are problematic in many schools, so an autistic young man who identifies as gay may be on the receiving end of bullying both because of his autism and because of his sexuality.

Some parents have specific views about sexuality which don't support a child who identifies as non-heterosexual or as transgender. While people are entitled to their beliefs, it needs to be considered that gender-diverse and sexuality-diverse young people are at significant risk of violence and aggression from others, and at higher risk of attempting or completing suicide than peers. Support from their family is essential to help them get through the difficult teenage years.

ISSUES WITH OTHER TEENS

Autistic and non-autistic young people tend to socialise differently and to have different kinds of peer relationships. Teens socialise with each other in a very different way than children do, and many autistic young people do not relate in the same way as their non-autistic peers. Some autistic teens are also shielded by their family from discussions of sexuality, so they are at a disadvantage when peers talk about sexual things. Autistic preteens and teens may seem naive and childlike because they have different interests, and this can result in social isolation or exclusion or bullying.

> When I was a kid, I did Irish dancing. The lessons were at school, and I would go on Saturday – I really enjoyed it. It was one of a small number of physical activities I was any good at! One time we had this competition with the other schools in the area. I would have been 11 or 12. While in the dance class I never got bullied, at the competition there were these mean girls who were a couple of years older than me.
>
> I hadn't got my period yet, but I did know about periods. I went to the bathroom and the mean girls were in there, doing whatever mean girls do. I saw a brown paper bag in the bin and said I wondered why someone had put their lunch in the bin. The mean girls thought this was hilarious and gave me a really

hard time. I eventually worked out what the brown bag was for, but I was really embarrassed when those girls teased me like I was a little kid. (Jenny)

RESILIENCE AND BULLYING

Sadly, bullying is all too common in schools and autistic preteens and teens are often on the receiving end of unwanted aggression and cruelty by fellow students. Bullying can occur in many settings, both in the physical environment of school and also online. Cyberbullying is particularly dangerous as it can mean that the child does not even feel safe at home. There is no doubt as to the impact of any kind of bullying, but it can be particularly severe when directed at impressionable children and young people. Bullying can result in low self-esteem, self-hatred, and outcomes such as post-traumatic stress disorder, depression, self-harm or suicide. Bullying is never okay and should not be tolerated or ignored in any setting. Autistic children and teens are likely to have social anxiety and difficulties being themselves at school. Bullying compounds this and can lead to a lifetime of self-doubt and self-hatred. Autistic people have a number of issues to contend with which can't be changed. Bullying is an additional problem, and one that is largely preventable.

While bullying experienced by younger children tends to be 'simpler' and involve name-calling or physical violence, as children get older the nature of bullying often changes. For older children and young teens, bullying may be focused around excluding or ridiculing the person. New 'topics' for bullying tend to arise toward the teen years as well, resulting particularly in homophobic and transphobic bullying. Bullying might be subtler at this stage and might be unnoticed by the autistic student in the immediate and short term. Realisation may hit later on, often causing embarrassment that feeds into self-hatred.

In my high school, there were these two boys, and they always used to call me Ralph Lauren. I thought they were my friends, whenever they saw me, they would shout 'Hey Ralph' or 'What'ya doing, Ralph Lauren?' Then they would laugh. It was only about 15 years later that I realised they were laughing at me not with me, and that they were being mean and teasing me because I never looked fashionable and Ralph Lauren was a men's fashion brand. I was so upset when I realised this, and it made me wonder what else I misunderstood at school. (Tom)

There are a number of issues that make bullying in school years difficult to address. These include:

- *Not knowing that it is occurring.* Many parents are unaware their child is being bullied, and many autistic children do not realise that they need to tell someone what is going on.

- *Invalidation or denial by school staff.* Some autistic young people complain to an adult of bullying, only to have their concerns dismissed or ignored. Sometimes they or their parents are given largely unhelpful advice, such as 'You wouldn't be bullied if you were more resilient.' While that statement is essentially true, it doesn't help a lot. Firstly, it is blaming the victim. It can be viewed as saying 'You need to change your own behaviour in order to stop the bully being aggressive to you.' It is also impossible to acquire resilience overnight. Such advice is a bit like saying to the child, 'If you grew ten centimetres taller overnight, you wouldn't be bullied.' That is also probably true, but is also impossible. Other dismissive comments can include statements like 'Just keep away from the bully.' A school yard is not a very big place, and bullies tend to find their victims quite easily. This is another example of victim-blaming.

- *Being too trusting.* Autistic children and teens can be very trusting. (This is true of many older autistic teens and adults also.) This trusting nature can be exploited by bullies, who will often ask the young person to do something under the guise of friendship or inclusion. The autistic teen – keen to make friends – will do some publicly embarrassing thing and be surprised when the apparent friendship with the bully results in them being ridiculed by their peers. This sort of bullying can occur on many occasions, with the autistic young person desperate to find approval. Such incidents can be further compounded if other children record them and share them online. This is an example of bullying that follows an unsuspecting autistic teen from the school yard to their home, and that can result in severe anxiety and shame. It is sadly all too easy to understand how bullying can lead to suicide.

- *Copying the bullies.* In some instances, autistic children and teens may themselves become bullies in order to be accepted by their peers.

- *Defending themselves.* Sometimes autistic children and teens are disciplined when they take matters into their own hands and fight back. Because autistic children tend to operate on one level and not to consider things like who is watching when they fight back, they may be disciplined while the bullies themselves get away with their behaviour.

- *Level of social skills.* It is important to note that bullying should not be seen as an inevitable result of autistic children's and young people's apparently less developed social skills. In the bully–victim relationship, it might be more accurate to see the person with the lower level of social skills as the bully.

- *Anxious preoccupation.* Children and young people who experience bullying may find that it occupies their thinking a lot of the time. School can be a place of terror, but adults may have no idea that this is occurring. Things like persistent school refusal may be a sign that bullying is occurring, as may your child being more anxious and overloaded at home.

- *Not reporting bullying.* It may not occur to autistic children and teens that bullying is going on, or they may have reported it and been given an unsatisfactory or unhelpful answer and decided there is no point trying to report it further. Given the significant damage to mental health and well-being that bullying can cause, it always needs to be addressed.

Bullying is a significant and complex issue often requiring many strategies and approaches to address. Autistic children and young people need to be protected, and they need to understand what they can do to strengthen their own ability to stay safe and that they can report bullying behaviour. Strategies to address bullying also need to address the behaviour of the bully, given that that is the key factor. Evidence shows that school bullies – and particularly boys – have poor outcomes as adults, including higher rates of unemployment, low school attainment, social exclusion and imprisonment. While it may be hard to sympathise with bullies, improving outcomes for them also benefits society through things like less criminal behaviour.

If your child is being bullied, it is important that you know this, that you report it to the school or place where it is occurring, and that you help your child to work through the issues the bullying has caused.

Bullying includes sustained or ongoing harassment, intimidation and social exclusion, as well as physical or verbal aggression.

Some actions can minimise the risk of bullying and can be helpful for some autistic preteens and teens. Being self-confident but not arrogant can minimise bullying that targets perceived victims in the school. Being visibly with other students in a friendship group can minimise opportunistic bullying. Gender- or sexuality-diverse students who are very open and comfortable with their diversity in a supportive school environment are less likely to be bullied than those who are struggling to accept their identity or who are in an unsupportive environment. Other useful strategies are joining a sporting team or learning a martial art. For example, not many school bullies are willing to take on someone who is a black belt in judo!

WHAT ARE PROTECTIVE FACTORS FOR RESILIENCE?

Much as there are risk factors that make it harder for a young person to acquire resilience, so also there are also some very effective protective factors. Where these are present, your child is more likely to build and maintain resilience.

Protective factors for resilience among autistic young people (and adults) include the following.

Self-acceptance

Accepting themselves and building their confidence can assist your child's ability to take on new challenges. Self-acceptance is an attitude which can be modelled by parents and other adult carers. This can be shown by a combination of demonstrating support for and valuing your child and also behaving in a way that demonstrates that you value yourself as well. Self-acceptance should be based on a clear awareness and understanding of one's own strengths and areas of struggle or difficulty in a non-judgmental manner. It is important not to confuse self-acceptance with the need to be perfect, which is impossible.

At high school the other girls kept asking me if I was a lesbian. I had no idea what they were talking about, as I didn't know what a lesbian was. After a couple of months Sarah told me that what she and I were doing when we were by ourselves meant

I was a lesbian. So, the next time one of the girls asked me, I said, 'Yes, I am a lesbian', and smiled at them. No-one mentioned it again. Since then, I have always been quite open and happy about using the lesbian word, and I have never been bullied about it. (Lara)

An assumption of competence

One issue that autistic people experience – and those with other health conditions or disabilities too – is an assumption by significant people in their life that they are incompetent or incapable of achieving what others do. This assumption is often driven by broader attitudes in society around autism. It starts from being something external to your child, but they will most likely internalise it and believe themselves less capable than their typically developing peers if they hear and see this attitude being expressed around or about them.

Contrary to this assumption of incompetence, you can instil in your child an assumption of *competence*. Instead of focusing on what your child can't do, build their confidence and self-perception that they are competent and capable. If they want to try something new, where possible support them in doing that. This does not mean ignoring their limitations, but it does involve challenging the widely-held view that all autistic children are unable to do what other children their age can do.

My parents always told me that I could do anything as long as I learnt how to do it and practised long enough. Even though I was devastated when I found out I couldn't be a pilot because of my vision not being good enough, I knew I could do so many other things. Some things I have had to do a lot more practising than others, like driving, I think I had twice as many lessons as most other people. Also, some things I found I didn't like doing much, like riding a bicycle, so I just stopped. I always felt loved and supported by my parents, even when no-one else seemed to really understand me. (Edward)

Social and emotional support

Children and young people who are – and feel – supported in family life and in social settings with friends or the family and relatives have a good base to build from in terms of their life skills, including resilience.

Social and emotional support are great protective factors for resilience. While a lack of emotional support from family is a risk factor for invalidation, social and emotional support can be a great validating factor.

Positive reinforcement for good work or positive behaviour

Positive reinforcement is a great protective factor around acquiring resilience. It can effectively build a positive self-image and confidence to try new things. Give your child positive reinforcement for good work or behaviour in different areas of their life (relationships with siblings, schoolwork, after-school activities, etc.). This does not mean you should ignore everything else, but that you should give praise when it is deserved, and note skills and concepts that your child needs to develop further. Over time you will gain an understanding of when your child is being deliberately defiant versus when they are not sure what to do and this was what led them to choose something inappropriate or that they are overloaded and unaware of the impact of their behaviour.

> My parents made me do chores around the house for my pocket money, and if I did them without having to be asked over and over, then I got some extra money. I wanted to buy this game, and I was saving up for it, and I realised if I did the chores when they were on the chart instead of putting it off, I could save up quicker. Now, as an adult I am pretty good at keeping the house clean and tidy, when some of my friends really struggle with that. I think it is because it became a habit, and I could see it made my mum happy when I would help out with cleaning and tidying. (Sara)

Caring and respectful friends

Your child may have some friends. Parents have very little say in who their child chooses as a friend, and this can cause concern, particularly as children grow older. Friends who are caring and respectful of themselves and your child can be a great protective factor for resilience, as they can model and share positive qualities with your child and provide support. As your child grows, you will need to help them build their sense of self-protection and to develop their 'radar' to recognise when peers are being friendly or are in fact bullying or being abusive to them. You can nurture supportive friendships by setting up activities that you know your preteen or teen and those friends will enjoy. This is one area where online gaming can be very positive as you can host gaming parties at your house, which enables you to check what your child is playing online and to facilitate some face-to-face interactions.

A supportive, safe and understanding home environment

A supportive and safe home environment where parents and siblings understand and respect the autistic child or teen provides a great start in life which will help to build resilience and self-respect. This home environment can be the basis of a 'place of safety' which will help to support them through their life – and resilience – journey.

Some level of responsibility

Resilience and responsibility are related. For a school-aged autistic child, the act of taking on responsibility can be a great way to scaffold resilience and social responsibility as they grow older. If they had chores as a younger child, these can be expanded to include more responsibility. If they have not had responsibility for chores in the past, this can be a good opportunity to build their confidence through being trusted and supported to do new things.

The kinds of activities autistic young people might find beneficial include helping with looking after pets, household chores or helping their parent/s with online activities. Such activities are beneficial for a number of reasons, including feeling part of the household, building skills that can transfer into school and later into workplaces, and teaching them some new skills – mostly 'soft' skills which are valued in settings such as school and the workplace.

> My mum kept chickens, and when I was younger I used to collect the eggs. As I got older, she asked me to do more and more for the chickens until eventually I was responsible for feeding them, cleaning the chicken coop, making sure they had water, collecting the eggs and clipping their wings so they couldn't fly away. I put this on my CV when I was looking for a job, as it showed I could be responsible. I also got some work looking after people's pets when they went away, because I could talk about how good I was with animals. (Rick)

Being stretched or challenged to do something new or more difficult

A protective factor for resilience is the idea of stretching your child to take on something a little more challenging or a new activity. In fact, this concept of stretching is at the core of acquiring resilience. A resilient person takes on new challenges or greater difficulty and learns from this. This in turn builds their ability to take on more challenges and not to be too concerned when new or more difficult challenges arise. The controlled challenges discussed in this book represent that stretching.

Things may not always go to plan with stretching. Sometimes the challenges will be too difficult, or your child will have a setback. However, that does not mean that you – or your child – should give up. Stretching and challenging needs to be done in a supportive manner, and if there is a setback, stop, debrief with your child, and reassess the approach. This kind of stretching and challenging is an ongoing activity throughout your child's life.

Having a positive self-identity as an autistic person

Many of the risk factors around resilience and autism stem from a lack of understanding of autism, prejudice against autistic people and/or focusing only on deficits. Autistic people can experience insecurity, self-doubt and self-hatred where they perceive autism negatively because of the things that they hear and the way that others treat them.

Helping your child to build a positive identity and self-perception as an autistic person is incredibly valuable. Not only does this impact on acquiring resilience, but it also has positive flow-on effects to almost every element of your child's life. Helping your child to view themselves in a positive light and to see autism as an intrinsic part of their character, with strengths and support needs like any other person has, is very helpful. This is preferable to having a child despising themselves for being different. These positive thoughts and attitudes are a pretty great gift you can give your child.

One of the ways that you can do this is by ensuring that they are aware of their autism-spectrum diagnosis, but also of a range of adults in the autistic community. This provides them with role models and demonstrates that autism is not a barrier to living a good and happy life. If your preteen or teen is non-verbal, it is important that they have access to information from and about non-verbal autistic adults and their lives.

Being able to navigate available services

It is important to be aware of what is available. There will be free or funded and private services available in most areas. Autism services are not 'good' just because they are free or because they cost a lot of money. It is important to evaluate not only what is available, but whether or not the service will support your child in developing their potential and without causing any unintended harm. Looking at the research evidence for different types of support services and strategies is very important. Anything that says it will 'cure' your child is unlikely to be of any benefit – there is no 'cure' for autism, nor is there any need for a cure. Also, anything that requires long-term commitment in terms of time and/or money needs to be carefully evaluated – is there an alternative that is more doable for you and your child?

Andrew Whitehouse, Winthrop Professor at the Telethon Kids Institute, University of Western Australia, has written extensively about how to choose support services for autistic children and teens. He recommends that you ask the provider the following questions:

- What is the therapy? You need to know what this therapy actually involves.

- What is the rationale of the therapy? You need to know why this therapy may be effective for your child.

- Is the therapy safe? You need to know that this therapy will not harm your child.

- Is the therapy effective? You need to know if there is scientific evidence that this therapy can lead to improvements.[5]

These questions are as relevant for younger children as they are for older children and teens.

Access to support and resources

- *Assessment.* Depending on where you live, different types of assessment will be required, or different providers will be required to complete the assessment, to allow you or your child

5   Whitehouse, A. (2016) *A Guide for How to Choose Therapy for a Child with Autism.* Available at http://theconversation.com/a-guide-for-how-to-choose-therapy-for-a-child-with-autism-64729 (accessed 5 December 2017).

to access funding for supports, whether these are for education, communication or similar. Check with your paediatrician, general practitioner or local autism organisation for relevant and up-to-date information around assessment processes and procedures.

- *Psychologists*. Psychologists may offer support services to promote positive mental health, well-being and resilience. These are usually most effective if the psychologist has a good understanding of the autism spectrum and is comfortable and skilled at communicating in an autistic-friendly manner. If you have an autistic daughter, it is particularly important to find a psychologist who has knowledge and experience in working with autistic girls, as there are still many clinicians with a poor understanding of autism in girls and women. This can cause issues in seeking an autism assessment and also in accessing effective clinical support and therapy for your daughter.

- *Psychiatrists*: Similar considerations apply as for psychologists, although psychiatrists can also prescribe psychiatric medications if these would be beneficial. This does not apply to all autistic children and young people. However, management of anxiety and/or depression can be more effective with psychiatric support in place.[6]

- *Public health services*. Public health services may offer a range of support services for autistic children, young people, adults and/or their families. These are often based in a case-management model and provide practical supports and well as clinical ones.

- *Books and blogs*. There are books and blogs around many aspects of autism. When reading these, it is important to ask whether or not they are accurate and useful. For example, if a blog focuses on 'curing' autism, the supports suggested are not likely to be helpful or effective.

- *Support groups – online and face-to-face – for parents and children.* These also can vary in quality and interaction style. Parent-run groups tend to have a different tone and focus compared with groups run by autistic adults. (Some are run by autistic adults who are also

---

6   Purkis, J., Goodall, E. and Nugent, J. (2016) *The Guide to Good Mental Health on the Autism Spectrum.* London: Jessica Kingsley Publishers.

parents to autistic children.) Autistic adult-run groups tend to use autistic communication styles: these are honest and to the point, and may seem confronting to people who are not expecting this.

- *Respite services.* To qualify for respite services, whether these are paid for or funded by your regional or national government, your child and family circumstances usually need to have been assessed by psychiatric and/or social work professionals. There are daytime, brief, overnight and longer-term respite services in many countries. Autism-specific respite services are often over-subscribed with very long waiting lists, and it may be that your child will receive as good a service from a non-autism-specific service, depending on their needs, age, interests, and so on.

- *Other parents.* Making connections with other parents to share what works well along the journey of raising your child can be a great support. It is important to note, though, that these connections are not always useful or helpful, especially if the other parents are stuck in a negative mindset. However, if you can offer each other mutual support, such as befriending your child's autistic friends' parents and providing social support for one another, this can have a huge positive impact on all the families.

- *Recommendations.* Parents of other autistic children and teens in your area or in social media groups can play a highly useful role in providing information about which psychologists, psychiatrists, occupational therapists and other clinicians, after-school programmes, GPs, dentists and other professionals have worked or not worked with their autistic children.

PROMOTING AND SUPPORTING INDEPENDENCE

Independence and resilience are closely related. For autistic young people, acquiring independence is one of the biggest challenges to successfully transitioning to adult life (whatever that may mean for the individual). Some autistics require a large amount of support from others in their day-to-day life, whilst others require very little support. Independence can be achieved no matter what your support needs are, it means that you have autonomy, that you control what happens in your life, rather than that you do everything yourself without assistance.

In the preteen and early teenage years children will often start trying to take steps towards more autonomy from parents and family life. These can range from small-scale departures from the family 'norm' to high levels of rebellion and defiance. A number of factors can impact on the extent of teenage rebellion and challenging of the family status quo. These can include difficulties with setting and understanding boundaries and limits, wanting to please and be accepted by new friends, or passions or interests that are focused on something negative or destructive.

The challenging and departing from family 'norms' that usually happens in the teen years, while often difficult for parents and their children, is in fact a vital part of the child building their sense of identity. It is important for parents to strike a balance between setting and enforcing appropriate boundaries while also allowing their child enough leeway to try new things and to build their autonomy. This is not easy and an approach that is effective with one child may not work at all with their sibling.

AUTISTIC PEERS AND ROLE MODELS

As children grow older, it is increasingly important for them to have a role model, a mentor or someone they admire to help them on a positive path to adulthood. Having friends amongst their peers who provide a positive influence is important as well. A positive influence would be a friend who promotes good choices, who doesn't model negative behaviour (such as self-harm or alcohol or other drug use), and who wants your child to succeed and be happy. Autistic children and young people can be particularly susceptible to following the lead of another person or group. They may have felt lonely and isolated and want to please their friend or their peer group in order to gain their approval and support. The fear of losing a friend or a peer group can outweigh concerns around whether or not what they are doing is safe. Coupled with the fact that autistic people tend to be quite trusting and naive – seeing everyone as though they view life as they themselves do – and also trustworthy, honest and kind. Sadly, we live in a world where many people are *not* trustworthy, honest or kind, and may be all too happy to prey on a young person who has those qualities. For this reason, building resilience and self-worth, together with the ability to set and keep boundaries, is very important. As most parents do, encouraging your child to identify positive role models and friends and social groups is an essential part of how you can support your autistic child in navigating the world safely.

It seems that if young people do not see adults who share their experience (in this case, autism) doing anything positive or engaging in the world, it is really difficult for them to imagine themselves in a positive place as adults. The notion that 'If you can't see it, you can't be it' applies here. It is therefore important for autistic young people to be exposed to autistic role models and, if possible, mentors. There are some renowned autistic people in a number of fields. They include people such as author and animal behaviourist Temple Grandin, author John Elder Robison, IT innovator Alan Turing, musician Susan Boyle and actor Dan Ackroyd. There are also some autistic characters or characters with autistic traits in popular culture. These include Legion in *Marvel Comics X Men*, Oskar Schell in the film *Extremely Loud, Incredibly Close* and Sheldon Cooper in TV show *The Big Bang Theory*. A role model doesn't even have to be a famous person or fictional character. If your child has a friend or family member with autism who sets a strong positive example, that person can be incredibly valuable in supporting your child's self-esteem and sense of autistic identity.

Some autistic children and young people have a sense of autistic pride and relate to adults who might be well known in the world of autism advocacy. This can be an excellent source of a positive focus and has the advantage that many autistic advocates are active – and approachable – on social media. Many teens and young adults gravitate towards autistic adults. The line between autistic teens focusing on positive influences and negative ones can be quite slim, however, and their focus can change many times over the course of their lives. Supporting your child's engagement with positive autistic roles models can help to propel them in a positive direction which will hopefully stay with them when they become adults.

The sense of difference experienced by many autistic teens is often seen as a negative – it may engender feelings of exclusion and isolation. They may feel that they are the only person in the world who experiences life as they do. The sense of isolation is all too often a reflection of their real experiences of being excluded by peers. Insults based around autism, neurodivergence and intellectual disability can be incredibly hurtful and can have the effect of the young person hating their autism and, by association, themselves. This in turn can damage the young person's sense of self and their capacity for self-esteem and resilience.

One way to nip this issue in the bud is to imbue the young person with a sense of autistic identity and autistic pride. Give your child the opportunity to meet and spend time with autistic peers and adult role models, and ensure that the messaging you give them around autism includes a lot of positives. Seeing their difference as a good thing has the added benefit of making it harder for bullies' insults to hit home, and also helps your child to value and like themselves just as they are.

WHAT DOES RESILIENCE LOOK LIKE AT THIS LIFE STAGE?

Resilience looks different at different points in a young person's journey to adulthood. It is something that can grow and evolve over time. The indicators that an older child or teen is building their resilience and has built a foundation for their ongoing path to resilience and independence include the following:

- They are more willing to try new things.

- They are less anxious about new activities and change.

- They have greater social confidence, and in particular the ability to say 'no' to peers who ask them to do something they do not want to do or that will damage their reputation.

- They are more able and willing to initiate new activities.

- They are more able to handle setbacks, mistakes and failing.

- They are more confident in who they are.

- They are more able to report and/or stand up to bullying.

- They have a more positive view of themselves.

- They have the capacity to think about the future in positive terms.

- They are more able to tell parents, teachers and other trusted responsible adults any concerns they may have.

For older children and teens on the autism spectrum, acquiring resilience can be very difficult but it is certainly achievable. You can help by supporting and putting in place protective factors and addressing risk factors, as well as by supporting them in liking and valuing themselves and in taking on stretching activities. This is a good way to start them on a lifelong path to resilience, independence and self-worth.

CHAPTER 3

AUTISTIC CHILDREN AGED 11–15

Strategies and Activities around Building Resilience

This chapter will focus on a range of life events and developmental milestones that autistic children aged from 11 to 15 years old are likely to experience. In each case it will include a description of the life event and the specific issues that might pose a challenge for autistic preteens and teens. Each milestone will also include information on what a good outcome might look like, as well as activities and strategies parents can put in place to help their child develop resilience and set the foundations for independence by successfully navigating through that life event.

The activities in this book may be of value to children of all cognitive abilities, including those who speak and those who use other communication methods. The activities may require some adaptation to be effective for your individual child. The activity outlines draw on the concept that 'Parents know their own children better than anyone else'. The activities and information in this book can be seen as a framework through which to understand and support your child rather than a prescriptive programme that must be followed exactly.

STARTING HIGH SCHOOL

Starting high school is one of the biggest single milestones that many preteens experience. Not only is the school itself new to them, but it may also be in a different and often an unfamiliar location, and offer a different environment. In addition, some of the subjects may be new, and all of the adults who teach these subjects will be new and unfamiliar. Children may never have moved around a school as much during the day or had to have so many different books and equipment.

Sometimes children's friends go to a different high school, which means that established friendships are not able to be maintained during the school day. Starting high school puts students who were the biggest and oldest in their primary school into the position of being the smallest and youngest. Bullying can occur, from new peers as well as from older students. There are different expectations for high-school students, with things like exams and independent studying, which might not have occurred in primary school, forming an important part of the school culture. The coursework is usually more difficult, and the environment of high school tends to be more formal and more rigorous than at primary school. Children who were good at a subject in primary school may struggle to keep up at high school. Even for non-autistic students the move to high school is a huge and often a frightening change. A student who has attended a special school and who is moving to a special high school will face many of the same challenges and anxieties around new people, new subjects and new environments.

Autistic students can struggle when faced with such a big change. They might be singled out by bullies or be excluded by classmates. The change to a new environment, a new curriculum and new teaching, administration and support staff alone can be enough to overload and disturb an autistic child. For this reason, it is very important to plan well ahead for the transition and, if you have a choice of school, to focus on the best fit for your child.

Autistic children may come to the attention of the school through behaviour that is deemed inappropriate. Sometimes this behaviour is the result of the child trying to navigate the very new world of high school, through self-soothing and stimming or through experiencing shutdown or meltdown in response to extreme anxiety. Any issues around coping that the child had at primary school can be multiplied greatly when they are placed in a new school environment. Given the magnitude of the transition to high school, a number of strategies may need to be applied to support your child at this critical transition.

I went to a small primary school. There were only about 100 kids, and it was a very supportive environment. We did lots of art and music. I actually really enjoyed primary school. I was rarely bullied and my talent for art was very much supported and rewarded.

When I went to high school, it was completely different. There were about 1000 students, and I was instantly hated. I never knew why that was and found that very confusing. Even the older year levels would torment and bully me. Within two weeks of going to this school, I figured out that I was different. I thought there must be something 'wrong' with me. And in addition to the bullying, we had to write with a fountain pen and we were marked on our handwriting. I couldn't write neatly with an ordinary pen but with a fountain pen, which seemed to spurt ink everywhere, I had a bunch of illegible essays. I had been looking forward to going to high school, so I felt really disappointed that it was so horrible. Thankfully my parents worked out what was going on with the bullying and sent me to a different school. It wasn't perfect but was much better. (Jenny)

ACTIVITIES TO HELP BUILD RESILIENCE AND CONFIDENCE AROUND STARTING HIGH SCHOOL

The transition to high school is a significant step. It is something that will almost certainly be challenging for your child and for you. It can help if you start preparing your child for high school well in advance of them going there.

Activity 1 – Getting to know the environment

Autistic children struggle with change in a variety of different ways. Going to a new place with a new teacher, new peers and new expectations is a significant challenge. Anxiety can be overwhelming, but can be addressed through messaging and understanding around starting school. Autistics tend to do better with change if they have an idea of what the new experience might involve. Younger children often benefit from social stories. The rationale behind social stories is essentially one of creating a mental road map for an autistic child in order to lessen the impact of change. However, older children may think social stories are a bit 'young' for them and may not engage well.

You can take the idea of a social story and create a road map for different elements of starting high school in a way that might appeal more to your child. This could include taking photos or videos of the physical environment of the school, or taking your child to visit the school a number of times prior to starting. This preparation will help to address anxiety about the physical environment. You can also take them to meet the teaching staff or the learning support unit staff at the new school. While this will not address every anxiety around the change, it may assist your child in managing the transition better. If you are able to make a number of transition visits, it is a good idea to make the first visit when no students are present, as the sheer number of students in high school can itself be quite overwhelming.

The next visit may be to meet some key teaching or support staff, and then a number of visits that build up the amount of time your child spends at the school may be helpful. However, it is worth bearing in mind that for some autistics not wanting to be seen as different may mean that they will only engage in visits that 'everyone' does, such as open days or formal whole-class visits.

Activity 2 – Open question session

This activity involves making a time for your child to ask any question they wish about high school. Give them some time to prepare and consider questions, and then sit down and have an 'interview' at which they can ask you anything they want to. Let them know there are no silly questions and that, to the best of your ability, you will answer everything they ask. This exercise can help give you a heads-up as to what may be problematic in high school, as it can give you a good idea of what your child is worried about. It is also a good preventive step in addressing your child's anxiety around the transition.

If your child can't think of any questions or has no idea of the differences between their current school and the next school, you may like to explore the high-school website together first. While you are exploring the website, you could point out some of the differences between the two schools. Prior to visiting, you may like to view the uniform on the web, look at canteen and lunch options, and the like.

Activity 3 – Rewards and recognition

This activity involves working with your child to decide upon a small reward for completing challenges related to starting high school.

Discuss the parameters of the reward or rewards with your child and make sure it is something meaningful for them. It will be different for every child. Work together to agree at what point the award should be given, what will trigger it (e.g. the length of time they have been at school, around attendance or around academic results). The purpose of this activity is to stretch your child's capability, to build their confidence, and to help encourage them to attend and stay at school. While the decisions around how the reward will work can be driven by your child, use your judgement to ensure that they are not setting too hard a challenge – or too easy a one, for that matter. If your child does not achieve what they set out to achieve, use that as an opportunity to talk about any issues and to work through what needs to be done to assist them in achieving their goal in the future.

Be aware that the reasons behind them not achieving their goal may be quite complex, and could be the result of something beyond your child's control. For example, it may be that your child is most scared about buying and eating lunch at the canteen because they have always had a packed lunch. Before setting up a reward for being able to do this, you may want practise at home and to pre-teach the skills required. In this case this would mean that you would need to teach how to choose from a canteen-style lunch display or menu system, and – depending on the school – paying and collecting change, if necessary, as well as picking up and carrying the food, opening containers, and the manners that should be used with the canteen staff.

Activity 4 – Communicating support needs to high-school staff

If your child has high support needs, there should be at least one transition meeting at which staff from both the current school and the new high school meet with you and your child to discuss strengths and support needs and strategies. However, if your child has less obvious or lower support needs, this sort of meeting may not always take place, and in that case your child may well have to communicate their own support needs to the high-school staff.

Most schools have some form of individual learning plan, and these vary considerably in their scope and usefulness. The plan should help to ensure that staff understand your child's support needs, but only once it has been written and distributed.

To help your child become confident in asking for support or for access to strategies that enable them to learn most effectively, you can ask them to take more responsibility for chores around the house, with which you will assist them *whenever* they ask or indicate that they need assistance. In addition, where possible delay providing things for your child until they communicate that they want them.

Activity 5 – What does your child want going forward?

(This activity is best used within the first six months of your child starting high school.)

This activity involves having a conversation with your child about what they want to happen in school. You can focus on areas such as friendships and socialising, curriculum and workload, and what would make them happier at school. This can be quite an abstract process. As many autistic people are more concrete thinkers, it may help if you prepare the conversation with some concrete examples to prompt their responses. Questions like 'Would you like to have more quiet time at lunchtime?' or 'What activities do you think you would like for quiet time?' may help. In some instances, what your child wants may not be possible. In others, it may be easily achievable.

Make it clear at the outset of this discussion that you may well not be able to make some of their wants happen, whereas others may be achievable. This kind of conversation can enable your child to gain more agency over their education. Some of the ideas generated may be things that might help other children too and, depending on the culture of the school and your relationship with the staff, these may be things that you could suggest they implement.

Other things to look at with your child are: What do they like (best)? What would they like (more) help with? Whom do they like? Is there anyone they are afraid of?

Signs that your child is managing the transition to high school well include:

- They are always or usually willing to go to school.

- They have a friend or friends at school.

- Their anxiety around school is minimal or decreasing.

- They are happy to share stories and experiences from school with you or other trusted adults.

- Their grades for subjects do not dip significantly.

- Your contact with their school is not only focused on managing issues; but when it is, the issues are resolved well and to your satisfaction.

HOMEWORK AND EXAMS

The academic load at high school can differ quite significantly from that at primary school. The focus of high school is often on the end result of further education or careers, even at the younger year levels. The structure of high school is different as well, which can be difficult for many autistic – and non-autistic – students to manage. There is a different level of discipline in high school, and often students are required to wear a uniform – and even where they are not, there may be a significant amount of social pressure to wear particular shoes or clothes. These things can all be challenging for autistic students.

There is often greater pressure on high-school students to perform, whether in a special or a mainstream school. This can come from teachers, but also from parents. When children get to high school, the pressure may get perceptibly more 'serious'. There are exams for many subjects and often there is considerably more homework. These changes may be quite overwhelming to autistic students and may cause significant stress. Coupled with the other changes outlined previously in this book, these may be quite a challenge. Children who were doing well academically may see a marked drop in their academic performance, leading to feelings of failure and insecurity. In addition, social confidence may dip as your child encounters an environment with new, and more, unwritten rules and social expectations.

ACTIVITIES TO EXPLORE DIFFERENT PERSPECTIVES
Activity 1 – Introducing perspective

One of the difficulties autistic people can experience is being 'in the moment' – instead, we tend to feel as if the 'now is forever'. While this can be seen as a positive, for many autistic people it means that they struggle to see where they are now in relation to how this might impact on the future. They may struggle to realise that a negative experience or feeling will pass and may feel 'stuck' with whatever is going on at the present moment. In terms of study, this means that autistic children and young people may struggle to understand that the fact that they are not proficient in something now doesn't necessarily mean they will *never* master it. Autistic children need to understand that just because they are having trouble with a subject now, that doesn't mean that they always will. This tendency can also mean that when they have a difficult interaction with a teacher or peer, they may assume that this will be the kind of encounter that they will *always* have with that person. This can lead to truanting and school refusal unless it is tackled quickly.

Unfortunately, we autistics tend not to believe 'now is forever' about good or positive experiences, but usually do for difficult experiences, which is where being 'mindful' – being in the moment and accepting it non-judgmentally as temporary – is so useful.

This activity involves talking with your autistic child about the past, the present and the future. You can use an example of something they struggled with when they were younger, and how they practised and worked to become proficient at it. It is a good idea to use an example around study or school so that they can relate it to their current challenge at school. For example, when your child started primary school they may not have been able to read and now they can, or they couldn't use Prolo2go or other AAC devices but now they can. Using the example from their past to explore how they overcame that difficulty earlier in their life, you can then link that experience to how they might manage the difficulty they are experiencing now. You can talk about some ways in which they might approach improving their capacity for schoolwork, taking their experience in younger life into consideration.

Activity 2 – Accepting other people's perspectives

One of the things many autistics struggle with is when people say one thing but mean another. At primary school they may have developed an understanding of their teacher, but then when they move to high school they have to learn a whole set of new teachers' communication styles, as well as those of all their new peers.

In this activity, you give your own perspective and guess your child's perspective on something you are eating, and vice versa. For example, you: 'I really like the colour and texture of this potato, and I think you do too – what do you think about the stew?' After your child has stated what they think, ask them what *they* think *you* think. Have this kind of conversation a number of times, and then deliberately get their perspective wrong. This can lead to an exploration of the reality that people may think and feel very differently about something, and that that is okay.

Signs that your child is managing the transition to high-school learning well include:

- They are realistic about understanding the challenges in transitioning to high school.

- They seldom or never have meltdowns or shutdowns around workload or academic performance.

- School refusal is less frequent or does not happen.

- There is less anxiety around academic performance.

- They demonstrate an understanding that it can take a while to learn new skills and the incremental nature of building confidence in schoolwork.

- They willingly engage in goal-setting and in evaluation of their learning.

MANAGING BAD NEWS

We all receive bad news from time to time. It can range in severity from getting a bad result in an exam, crashing the iPad or Xbox, to finding out about the death of someone we love and care about. Autistic children and young people can struggle with receiving bad news, as can everyone. Because receiving bad news is an inevitable part of life, it is important to equip autistic young people with the ability to manage, and to develop coping strategies for disappointment and bad news. Resilience around receiving bad news is a very useful attribute, but it can be hard to achieve.

Bad news is often anxiety-inducing, and that may compound the impact the next time the young person receives bad news. (This is the *opposite* process to building resilience.) For autistic young people, one issue with bad news can be the issue of not knowing the appropriate response. Autistic young people may believe that there is a 'right' response to receiving particular bad news, but they are not sure what it is or how to express it. This can cause significant anxiety in itself, in addition to that which occurs in response to the news. If an autistic child has been criticised for 'lacking empathy' or told that they respond inappropriately, they may be anxious around that, too, and that may result in them behaving in a way that is perceived by others as inappropriate, thereby compounding the issue. In fact, there is *no* 'right' way to receive bad news. Everyone responds differently to being told something devastating. Having a 'norm' of behaviour and insisting that children adhere to it in these kinds of situations may actually be very unhelpful.

> When I found out my friend died, I just sat on the floor and cried and howled for about four hours. I sounded like a wolf, I don't know where the sound came from, and I didn't know how to stop. But then, it all just stopped, and I wasn't even really sad, it was just like he had gone and that was it. But then when my grandpa died, I didn't cry at all, he was so sick and had been suffering for so long before he died that I just felt relief that he didn't need to suffer any longer. My mum said I overreacted to my friend's death and underreacted to my grandpa's death, but I was just being me. (Eddie)

Some parents shield their children from bad news. This is fine if the bad news is what is showing on the television news, about wars and crimes and other graphic violence, but shielding is less helpful when it is news that they will find out anyway. Matter-of-factly explaining to your child that something unpleasant has happened, and explaining what the implications might be for them and your family, is a good approach. Many autistic young people become understandably resentful if information they need to know is kept from them.

> When I was 12, my grandpa died. It was the day before my birthday, and I had a friend sleeping over. I remember my dad coming into my room and telling me. I loved my grandpa, but my main worry was that I didn't know what I was 'supposed' to do. I had seen movies and read books where someone dies, and the people left behind all did the same sorts of things, but

I didn't feel like grieving the same way they did. My love and empathy is more intellectual than emotional. While I understand this now, back when I was 12, I just thought I was horrible and cold-hearted for not crying or anything like that. (Jenny – 'What's the right way to grieve?')

ACTIVITIES AROUND RECEIVING BAD NEWS
Activity 1 – 'It's okay to…'

This activity is essentially a conversation that can occur at any time, whether or not bad news has just been received. The conversation centres around how responses to a traumatic event are different for each person and that this is okay. Explain to your child that, as long as their response does not involve violence or self-destructive behaviour, however they respond to bad news is okay. Introduce the idea that each person – autistic and non-autistic alike – has their own unique way of responding to bad news and that this is okay. Encourage questions and address any concerns.

When you are watching TV or a movie together, you can talk about how different characters respond to bad news, and compare and contrast these reactions to how you and/or other family members deal with bad news.

Activity 2 – Gaining perspective

Some autistic people worry a lot about bad things happening, often including things that others may not perceive as an issue. While the worst kind of bad news will get a similar response from most people, autistic children and young people may experience bad news and disappointment about things that others think are insignificant. This often results in invalidation of the autistic child if others tell them they are worrying unnecessarily about 'unimportant' things. In fact, the reaction from the child is an indication of how much the news or event impacts them. They are not 'overreacting', because for them the event *is* traumatic. Parents or other responsible adults belittling their experience is very unhelpful.

When I was 12, I became really worried about nuclear war. No-one I knew was worried about this, but I couldn't understand why we had nuclear weapons if there was no possibility of them ever being used again. Teachers telling me I was ridiculous just made me more upset, because I went and did a heap of research about nuclear testing and bombs and all the problems they cause. (Fiona)

If your child is extremely distressed by things that upset them while no-one else is, this too is unpleasant for them. Telling them that their worries are unimportant is not the way to address this and will most likely add to their distress. It is more helpful to work through their anxiety and to support and validate them. You can talk about perspective with your child and compare the consequences of different events. A good approach is to look at the impact of the event on them in real terms. Helping them to reflect on the magnitude of an event and its impact on them can help to guide them in how much they need to worry. This can be difficult because their response to apparently minor negative news and occurrences is genuine. It may take a while to instil perspective, but doing so can help your child avoid considerable misery. For that reason, this may be an ongoing activity.

> When I crash my computer, I get so upset, I scream and yell and used to throw things. My dad was really nice and helpful – he spent a long time helping me to understand that if I was able to not throw things, I could spend that time rebooting the computer instead, and it would be working again much quicker. Plus, now I don't upset Mum by breaking stuff when the computer crashes. Dad timed how long it took to reboot after each crash and what I was doing. It was so much quicker if I only scream and yell than if I broke things. Not yelling doesn't make it quicker though! (Joe)

Signs that your child is responding resiliently when managing bad news include:

- They have less generalised anxiety around negative things happening.

- When bad news is received, their responses are less severe and/ or less intense.

- They can talk about bad news with you or other trusted adults.

- They have increasing capacity to recognise the true the magnitude of adverse news and events and to respond accordingly.

PUBERTY CHANGES

Many autistic young people seem to experience puberty quite differently from their peers, who have one puberty such that biological, emotional and social changes all occur in one time period. Instead, autistics tend to have their biological puberty first – this does impact their emotions, but not in quite the same way. Whilst going through biological puberty, autistic young people experience all of the changes in body shape, hair growth, and so on. This can be very confusing for them, unless they are well prepared. In addition, for some young people who are gender-questioning or transgender, puberty can be an especially traumatic time. Statistically, there are proportionally more non-binary-gender autistics than non-autistics, so it is worth considering whether this is a journey with which your child needs support.

Menstruation – periods – is usually the most difficult aspect of biological puberty for girls, though some really struggle with their breasts developing as this impacts the way their body feels, comfortable sleeping positions and clothing. For boys, unexpected erections and wet dreams can be the most difficult aspects of this time of life.

Many parents struggle with discussing these kinds of things, but it is vital that autistic preteens and teens get accurate information so that they are not distressed by these changes to their bodies. If you are not comfortable talking to your child about these things, or if their receptive language makes it difficult to discuss such topics, you may like to use drawings or watch videos or cartoons about puberty and puberty changes. In particular, you will need to find a way to address how your child should manage periods or erections and wet dreams.

ACTIVITIES AROUND THE EXPERIENCE OF PUBERTY
Activity 1 – Sharing information

Share information with your child in a form that is meaningful to them. You can also show them photos of you or other family members pre- and post-puberty, so that they can see more general changes such as getting taller. Make sure to be very explicit about how their body will change over the next few months and years. Try to convey that, over time, the changes become the new normal.

Activity 2 – Getting comfortable with explicit information

Your child is likely to need support in understanding with whom they can share explicit information in regard to puberty. To minimise risks to them, it is important that they learn about the concept of privacy in relation both to their communication and their body, whilst understanding the protective and helping role of parents and teachers. You may want to think about who you would be comfortable with your daughter or son talking to about how to manage periods or erections! This activity is really for you, rather than for your child, though they are an important part of the activity.

Firstly, find some information for your child relating to their periods, erections or wet dreams. Then work out how you are going to convey this information to them. You may want to have some tampons or pads with you, if you are going to talk about these. If you are a single dad, this may be very difficult. However, if you are awkward or anxious when you discuss this with your daughter, she will be unlikely to come to you for help. It may be helpful to think about your daughter's sensory issues and motor skills to decide whether pads or tampons are likely to be more suitable for her in managing her periods. Will she need a reminder when to change her pad/tampon, and if so how will this happen? Will she remember how to dispose of the used pad/tampon, or will she need a visual schedule? Some families choose to consider an intrauterine device (IUD), which is a small contraceptive device that is put into the uterus (womb) to prevent pregnancy. The main reason for doing this is not as a contraceptive, however, but because it can suppress periods for a young person who is unable to manage them. IUDs can be removed when a young person wishes to conceive a child. Other options can include contraceptive implants.

If you have a son, you will need to find some information about erections and wet dreams and their unpredictable nature! Again, it is important not to be embarrassed when discussing these, but simply to be factual and honest. If talking is not appropriate, there are a number of resources that may be useful for you and your son. (See the Useful Resources section at the back of the book).

The final part of this activity is to create a plan with your child about how to manage their periods, erections or wet dreams. This plan may be a visual schedule with first/then, or it may be a set of written dot points or a cartoon – whatever works.

Activity 3 – Safety and sexual expression

Bullying can be exacerbated if young people do things that are perceived as sexually inappropriate, such as masturbating in class. With biological puberty, some autistics discover the pleasure and calming nature of masturbation, whilst others do not develop an interest in touching themselves in this way for many more years. As parents, it can be hard to perceive our growing children as sexual beings, but it may be devastating for a young person to be accused of being sexually inappropriate. This means that before your child starts to explore their body you need to have worked with them on the concept of privacy, and what is okay to do in private, or with someone special when they are older, rather than in public.

Your child may like to touch people's hair or other parts of their body, but as they move into adolescence this may be seen as sexually deviant. This means that you need to work with them on the concept of 'personal space' – whom they can touch, in what ways, when and where!

> Following a presentation on sexuality that I did, a parent came up to talk to me about her son. She was devastated because he was being accused of being sexually deviant, because he liked to touch the arms of girls who were much younger than him, just as he had done to try and get people to play with him when he was a primary school child. Unfortunately, he was now an adult and did not understand that society deems it unacceptable for an adult to be trying to play with and touch young children. Sadly, the only advice I could offer was to teach him not to touch any young girls. I have also had parents very concerned about their children masturbating in school. On discussion, most of the young people were self-soothing and unaware this was not an appropriate place to use this strategy. Explicitly teaching where this was okay and where it was not helped all these young people to be kept safe and prevent further bullying by peers. (Emma)

> When I was a teenager, I discovered masturbation, and I loved it – I didn't care if I was touching myself or if it was someone else. Because I had never learnt that sex and masturbation were supposed to be private things, I was doing things in really stupid places like the bus station! It was only once I had finished university that I learnt about privacy and the law and stopped

doing this. I think all young people, autistic or not, need to know about the law and sexual activity. (Mina)

SOCIAL/EMOTIONAL PUBERTY

In autistics, social/emotional puberty tends to occur much later than biological puberty, though this does not mean that sexual interest is not already there. This becomes apparent as the social gap between an autistic and their peers grows dramatically as their peers start dating and jostling for popularity, whilst the autistic young person is still focused on their passions and interests. Some autistic teens can become fixated on being popular and may really struggle emotionally if they are not. For autistics with a talent in any area, showcasing this talent may lead to a friendship group and an element of popularity. Other young people may stop wanting to be popular once they realise how much effort would be involved in seeking and maintaining popularity.

> I really wanted to be popular, and when I was starting high school I really bugged my mum about this. She told me that if I wanted to be popular, I would need to make sure my clothes and hair were exactly how other people thought they should be every day and this was just the beginning of trying to be popular. Clothes and hair have never interested me, so I decided that being popular was probably much too much hard work. Mum told me that instead I should find the geeks and the nerds and that they would like me for who I am and even better would probably like some of the same things I like. She was right, and even though I finished school five years ago, I am still friends with the geeks and nerds that I made friends with in my first year at high school. (Rob)

LETTING GO OF UNHELPFUL ACTIVITIES (E.G. INTERNET ADDICTION)

Everyone — autistic and non-autistic alike — has, or has the potential to have, some unhelpful behaviours. For adults, such behaviours might involve drinking alcohol at a risky level or gambling too much. These kinds of behaviours often arise in response to a difficult time in one's life or to past trauma, especially to events that occurred during one's formative years. Addictions and maladaptive coping strategies offer an escape, but they can be very damaging and can have a large and negative effect on a person's relationships, work and enjoyment of life.

Children and young people, including those who are autistic, may also have maladaptive coping strategies. These are often things like internet addiction, 'acting out', binge eating or anorexia. These strategies are ways in which people try to numb the pain of life or to create a psychological space in which they feel more in control. Doing something that seems pleasurable is seen as a good way to address unpleasant feelings and thoughts. Many people develop maladaptive coping strategies as a response to trauma or invalidation. Sadly, for our autistic children and young people, these invalidating and traumatic situations may have happened from a young age and can be severe. Bullying and even some unhelpful 'therapies' can cause trauma that may result in maladaptive coping strategies as a child grows through teen and young adult years.

Issues often start when an activity is pleasurable and offers temporary relief from stress and inner turmoil. For example, a parent might give a child an iPad when they are anxious or overwhelmed. The iPad does the job wonderfully – online games are immersive, engaging and a great escape from difficult times. Every time the child is stressed or upset, their parent gives them the iPad, or they ask for it. From then on, whenever the child is stressed, they make sure they get the iPad, whatever that may take…and at some point, for many young people playing games on the iPad is all they want to do. The online world is controllable and predictable. There is excitement and engagement to be had. There are some autistic young people who no longer attend school because of internet addiction, and teens who don't sleep at night but stay up playing online games and are unable to do anything else. Of course, those are quite extreme examples, but this is a real issue for many autistic young people and their families.

Blaming the technology – or the parent – is simplistic and unhelpful. A person who does not need an escape from managing a very difficult young lifetime can quite happily play a game online and then put the device away. Addiction is not so much a heightened interest in the addicting behaviour or substance – rather it is a response to a range of troubling experiences and emotions or a reliance on the addiction to feel good. It should be noted that giving your child a device is not inherently a bad idea. Many people drink alcohol and are not alcoholics. The issue is not the device itself, but what it offers somebody who needs an escape from the 'real' world. While setting boundaries around screen time is a very good idea, internet addiction is a specific issue which is related to, but different from, setting boundaries around internet usage. That being said, being aware of how long your child is online – and what they are viewing – is obviously a very good idea, and can help alert you to the possibility that the device is having a damaging impact. Checking the browser history can prevent young people having access to websites that you would rather they didn't. Many families find that it is necessary to have the computer or device in the family room or living room, and not in the young person's bedroom.

It is also important to be aware of the impact of addictive behaviours. Imagine a 15-year-old with an internet addiction. In practical terms, this addiction will probably impact things like school attendance and working towards employment and/or further education. Addiction also takes a toll on motivation and self-worth. Occurring at such a formative stage in life, this can be a significant risk factor for not completing school, attending further education or finding work. Such an addiction therefore compounds the issues already faced by autistic people around education and employment. The longer the addiction goes on for, the more damage it tends to cause to independence and resilience.

With internet addiction there are some handy strategies that minimise harm. If your child plays a lot of online games, they could learn how to create games themselves and learn coding, which could help them to be more engaged and potentially to earn an income through that skill at some point. However, that only addresses one part of the problem. A more holistic approach might include not only teaching coding but also working on the factors that resulted in the young person needing to 'run away' into the online world.

Autistic young people can be especially susceptible to addictions and maladaptive behaviours because they can become quite fixated on the behaviour. It may become an incredibly strong focus, almost like a negative passionate interest. As with other, more positive passionate interests, the addiction can become all-consuming, to an even greater extent than it might for a non-autistic person. If the behaviour is bound up with teenage rebellion, this can be extremely difficult to address. However, it *can* be addressed, and many autistic people have worked through their addictions and gained insight. The experience of overcoming an addiction – once the person has taken some control and made the decision to seek help to overcome it – is often very positive and affirming, and can impact significantly on building resilience and self-confidence in other areas of life.

If your child has an issue with addiction, in many cases the best practice is to do some work on where the addiction has stemmed from. This book can only offer a little advice on this matter: it is advisable to seek help from a psychologist or psychiatrist. Each individual is different. There are not many activities we can write here to address this issue. The lessons around resilience in relation to addiction and maladaptive behaviours are to work with the child to address the immediate issue (often through therapy) and also to help them transfer their learnings into the rest of their life. Another very important thing to be aware of is whether anything is happening at the present time or has happened in the past that is impacting on their life. You may not be successful in helping your child get through a difficulty with internet addition if the root cause – for example, anxiety around bullying at school – is still there. People who feel supported and validated do not generally develop addictions, so the aim is to help your child feel supported, validated and able to be happy in themselves as much as possible.

ISSUES WITH BULLYING

Despite many advances in education for autistic children in recent years, there is still a significant problem of autistic children being bullied – in school, in out-of-school activities and online. Bullying is experienced by a majority of autistic children, although statistics vary from country to country. Bullying often has a devastating effect on mental health and well-being, on self-esteem, on self-confidence and on identity, not only in the immediate aftermath but also long-term.

Starting high school can be a difficult time for autistic students, and one of the issues they often face is being singled out by bullies. There is a wide range of unhelpful responses to bullying. Statements like 'Your child wouldn't be bullied if they got some resilience', 'Just stay away from them' and 'Don't provoke them' are all examples of unhelpful responses that essentially represent victim-blaming and dismissiveness. These attitudes demonstrate a view that the autistic child is somehow responsible for the behaviour of the bully.

It is possible to address bullying, but it is necessary for the parent/s and the school to know what is going on and for the school to be willing to address the issue. Bullying can lead to disengagement from school,

school refusal, self-harm, addictive behaviour and severe anxiety, and can hasten the onset of depression and suicidal ideation and acts. It is something that always needs to be taken seriously.

Exercise – bullying

Imagine you are autistic, 12 years old and have just started high school. You don't really have any friends at the new school. There is one person you know, a girl who went to your primary school with whom you had a very difficult time. This girl became popular when you both started high school. You did not. The girl spreads rumours about you and tells your classmates about embarrassing things you did when you were a little kid. Within a short time, your experience of school is no longer pleasant or interesting. It is like a battleground. Lunchtime and recess are like something out of *Lord of the Flies*. You try to find somewhere quiet at lunch and recess where nobody will spot you, but every time you go to a classroom or the library the teachers tell you that you aren't allowed in there during lunchtime. The only pleasant thing at school is when you get to write fan fiction stories in English. Aside from that, the whole school experience is misery, with kids from all year levels ridiculing and teasing you. After a few weeks you tell your home room teacher about the bullying. She says 'Oh, just keep away from them.' You have been trying to do that, but unsuccessfully. You tell your mum, and she says the boys behave that way because they find you attractive. Both these pieces of advice from trusted adults are so unhelpful you never mention bullying to an adult again. You feel completely alone at school and wish you didn't have another five years of schooling to go.

Questions

- What were some of the problems in the school environment other than the bullying?

- Which attitudes of adults were unhelpful? How could they have been improved?

- What could the school have done to help address the bullying?

- Whose 'fault' do you think the bullying was? On whom would the school need to focus to address the issue?

- How could the school and parents support the autistic child to build their confidence and self-worth?

ACTIVITIES SUPPORTING RESILIENCE AND COPING STRATEGIES AROUND BULLYING

Activity 1 – Self-esteem list

Bullying impacts on several aspects of a child's character and mental state. One of the worst effects of bullying is the impact it can have on self-esteem and on the child's sense of their own worth. Low self-esteem is a terrible thing to carry: it can impact on a child's resilience and independence and can mean that they struggle to complete their education, join the workforce or engage socially with others. It can also form part of poor mental health and all that comes with that. Whether your child is being bullied or not, their self-esteem is a really important part of supporting their resilience.

For this activity, talk to your child about what kinds of positive attributes people can have. You could ask them to make a list. You could add a few attributes if you think this is needed (for example, if their list is sparse or if some of their responses are not very positive). Then, with your child, work down the list and point out the positive attributes that they themselves have that they have listed. You can talk about people or characters your child admires, and how they share attributes with your child.

Activity 2 – Tell me, tell you

A lot of autistic children who are being bullied may not tell their parents about this, for a number of reasons. One common reason is that they don't realise they can bring information like this to a parent. If nobody has *told* them to report bullying – and expanded on what 'bullying' actually means in practical terms – they may not share important information with their parents or teachers.

For this activity, start a conversation with your child around people in your life and theirs. Ask them questions to gauge their experience of others, such as whether they like being around that person – what they feel like or what they think when they are around that person. You could also share some of your own thoughts about people. You could even take turns, with you saying something about a person and then asking your child to say something. Through this activity you may be able to ascertain your child's experience of a range of different people in their life. You can use this basic format for talking about many people in your child's life, including people in school.

You should stress at the outset of the first 'tell me tell you' conversation that everything you and your child says is in confidence, but be sure to include the caveat that if someone has said they will hurt your child, another person or themselves, you may need to share that information with other adults to keep everyone safe. Make sure you do not – intentionally or inadvertently – betray your child's trust except in these circumstances, as this could easily destroy their trust in you.

INDICATIONS OF BULLYING

The one key sign that your child is *addressing* the situation of being bullied is that they are able to tell you or another responsible, trusted adult that they are being bullied. As bullying for autistic kids tends to be entirely one-sided, strategies should be more focused on addressing the bullying rather than trying to get your child to change their own behaviour.

In cases of bullying, the problem behaviour is most often the behaviour of the bullies themselves. However, some autistic students do engage in bullying behaviour, often at the behest of their 'friends'.

If your child suddenly stops wanting to go to school, this is usually an indicator that something negative has happened to them or around them, and bullying is one possibility.

BOYFRIENDS, GIRLFRIENDS AND CRUSHES

While autistic preteens and teens may mature later than their typical developing peers in terms of sexuality and interest in relationships, they may also have the same sorts of interest in sex and relationships as others do. There is a myth that autistic people are all asexual: while many are, most autistic adults are interested in sexuality and relationships.

In high school, young people often have a crush on somebody – usually a classmate or another child of a similar age. Some autistic children also may find themselves attracted to another person at school. Autistic young people often don't have as good a knowledge of the sort of unwritten rules about dating as their typically developing peers. They also might see games and teasing and think that these are the same as relationships. One of the authors remembers that in Year 7 the boys were showing girls a screw and saying, 'Do you want me to give you a screw?' (meaning have sex with them, rather than give them the actual hardware screw). She thought this was how you asked someone out, but soon realised from people's reactions that it didn't work that way.

Asking classmates on a date is often quite terrifying, for autistic and non-autistic children alike. They may be rejected, and then that rejection may result in bullying and teasing. But the impact can be even harder for autistics. Crushes and relationships in the preteen and teen years tend to be fairly fleeting and shallow, but autistic children may place more value on them. While many young people will break up with their 'partner' and move on almost straight away, for autistics the experience can be devastating.

Autistic young people may also be less aware of the potential for exploitation and abuse by adults. This can be combined with a naivety and thinking that everyone is as trustworthy as the autistic person is. For this reason, teaching self-protection and self-defence to autistic young people is a very good idea. Some parents are reluctant to 'scare' their child with a conversation about abuse and predation by paedophiles, but the fear experienced in a controlled environment with a parent explaining safety and self-protection is obviously far less distressing than the terror and lasting impact and trauma of the child who is actually preyed upon.

The kind of information around dating that is found online and on TV, in movies and in books, is often focused on adult sexual relationships. This can cause difficulties for autistic children and young people, who may equate what they themselves might be expected to do in a relationship with the actions of adults in popular culture. This can cause issues, especially when it comes to sexual behaviour. Autistic children and young people can struggle with boundaries and relationships and may behave in ways that seem inappropriate, such as calling their crush 100 times a day because they have seen this behaviour either in popular culture or between people in love and thought that is what you do in a relationship.

A greater proportion of autistic people are gender-diverse and/or have non-heterosexual sexual interests. Emerging research shows that gender dysphoria and transgender identification are considerably more common for autistic people than for neurotypical people. One study showed that gender variance was found to be 7.59 times more common in autistic children than in the neurotypical control group. Research also shows that higher numbers of autistic people identify as genderqueer, pansexual or non-binary than their neurotypical peers.[7] Sexual and gender identification are things that tend to occur in the preteen and teen years. Coupled with puberty and all that that entails, plus thinking about and developing their character and identity, the realisation of sexuality and gender identity can be a huge challenge for autistic young people. The challenge comes not only from the difficult and intense sorts of feelings and thoughts that arise as they come to terms with their gender and sexuality, but also from the kinds of reactions they may receive from peers. Homophobic and transphobic bullying is sadly all too common, and this can be a dangerous time for autistic young people. Those who identify as lesbian, gay, bisexual, transgender or queer and those who are questioning such issues are at a considerably higher risk of suicidal ideation and acts. Combine that risk with risks related to bullying and ableism, and autistic young people can be in a very difficult and dangerous space.

As a parent, it is vital that you support your child. For parents who have strong views around gender or sexuality, this can be understandably difficult. However, for your child's 'place of safety' to function, you need to work through your issues as soon as you can so that you can support your child. It may be a difficult learning experience for you, but it needs to be done. Your child's life is worth more than any discomfort you may have around their sexuality or gender identification.

When I was 15, I had a sexual encounter with an older man. It wasn't quite rape, but it also wasn't quite consensual – one of those sorts of very confusing and intense 'grey areas' in sexual behaviour. I was very upset by this encounter. Coupled with the fact I have always found men physically repulsive – beards and hair and sweat – yuck – the whole thing was traumatic and led me to think about my own sexual interest. As I like being around women, and they have soft skin and often have quiet voices, I figured I must be gay. Being an honest Aspie I talked to my

---

7   Andreus, J. (2015) *Autism and Diversity: Sex, Gender and Sexuality.* Available at www.vercida.com/uk/articles/autism-and-diversity-sex-gender-and-sexuality (accessed 5 December 2017).

parents about my sexuality. At the time, both of them belonged to a very conservative church. They aren't bad people at all, but they did not respond well to this news. I don't think I had even a brief conversation with my dad for over a month after my coming out. Not only did I feel conflicted in terms of my sexual identity, I also felt I couldn't talk to anyone about it.

Thankfully my mum was really supportive, and my dad came around and worked through whatever issue he had. They were always really prudish, but they were prudish about heterosexual things as well. When I see all the activism and promotion of sexuality and gender diversity, it makes me really happy because it means people are more understanding and less likely to be bigoted. I think supporting young people who are working through their sexuality and gender identity is much more helpful than just telling them it's wrong and leaving them to work out what's going on without that support from their parents. (Amber)

The key messages for parents to pass on to their children around dating, sexuality and crushes include these:

- *Teach them about consent.* If need be, give examples or role-play.

- *Offer non-judgemental acceptance.* Teach them that how they identify in terms of their gender and their sexuality is okay, and you accept them as they are. If they were born male and want to identify as female or vice versa, support this. There are some great resources on this topic, including the books *Transitioning Together* by Wenn and Beatrice Lawson and *The Autism Spectrum Guide to Sexuality and Relationships* by Dr Emma Goodall. Generally, this is not a 'phase' but part of their identity.

- *Be available to talk.* If possible, be the person they can talk to about issues around crushes and dating. As children mature, they need advice to a greater extent than they need instruction. Giving support and advice and being their adult friend and ally is a great spot to be in, and will help your child and support your ongoing relationship with them.

Signs that your child is managing well with emergent sexuality, crushes and dating include:

- They confide in you about crushes and about what is going on in terms of dating.

- They can talk to you or other trusted adults about their thoughts and concerns around dating, partners and sexuality.

- They are able to decline an offer from a prospective boyfriend or girlfriend.

- They are able and willing to discuss with you and with others ideas around gender and sexuality, and in particular how those ideas relate to them.

- If their boyfriend or girlfriend breaks up with them, they manage this with minimal fixations; but if they do become fixated, they respond to your direction and advice about what behaviour is appropriate and what might be seen as stalking.

ACTIVITY AROUND BOYFRIENDS, GIRLFRIENDS AND CRUSHES – OPEN FORUM

'Advertise' in your household that there will be an open forum on dating and boyfriends and girlfriends. Explain to your autistic child that this will be a place where they can ask any question and make any comment they want about dating, boyfriends or girlfriends, and related topics. Encourage them beforehand to think about what they want to know, and suggest that they write down questions in preparation. Tell them you will answer anything they ask, no matter how potentially embarrassing, icky or silly it might seem. Ask your child who they want to be involved in the forum, and assure them it will only be them and the person they select. This means that if they are embarrassed at the thought that siblings or other members of the household might be there, they can be comfortable in knowing it will only be people they select. You might also want to arrange activities for siblings to ensure they don't wander in mid-forum!

USING PUBLIC TRANSPORT OR TAKING A SCHOOL BUS

As children grow older, it can be helpful to support them in using public transport or the school bus. There is no 'right' age to do this: this is a situation where you should use your parental judgement to determine if your child is ready. When my generation were kids, you got put on the school bus with no support or preparation. This was not an ideal state of affairs. There are a number of issues around taking the school bus or public transport to school. Both the child and the parents can be very anxious around this, and often for good reason. School buses in the past and now can be a place where bullying may occur out of the sight of teachers or parents, with the only adult present being the bus driver, who can't really supervise or do a lot at the time should any incidents occur.

Aside from concerning behaviour by other passengers, taking a bus can be confusing for autistic children who may not know when to get off or may be overly anxious about missing stops. They may struggle with the idea of where to sit. Should they sit in the same seat every time or is it okay to chop and change? Going from a parent's warm and very private car to a bus full of other kids who may be unpredictable can be very stressful indeed.

Your child may have heard stories about incidents on the school bus or public transport from siblings or peers and this may add to their anxiety. Autistic children are often highly sensitive to parental feelings and stress and may therefore have picked up on your anxiety, making the experience of taking a bus or train for the first time that much worse. When it comes to new or different situations, children often take their lead from parents. While containing your own anxiety may be difficult, it can sometimes help if your child sees your confidence in them, not your fear – although this can be very hard, especially with children who are hyper-empathetic.

The best outcome is that your child is able to make the transition to using public transport or the school bus well; that the environment on the bus is friendly and safe; and that through this experience of making the move from going to school with a parent to going by themselves, your child builds their resilience and confidence. In most circumstances, it is not appropriate for a parent to ferry their child around everywhere they want to go, and long into adulthood. The transition to using the school bus or public transport is a very important step in their progress towards resilience and independence and to prepare them for adult life.

Signs that your child is managing well with taking the school bus and/or using public transport include:

- They are willing to start using the school bus or public transport, and then to continue doing so.

- When they talk about the bus trip, their comments are largely positive or neutral.

- They do not refuse to use the bus, or refuse less often.

- When you take them to the stop, they are willing to board the bus.

- When talking about school, they may mention the bus trip and speak about it without frequent negative comments or significant anxiety.

- If they have a passionate interest in transport, then the school bus becomes part of their general discussion around buses and trains, and the discussion is not negatively focused.

- They express wanting to go on buses or trains outside the context of the trip to school and/or do not respond negatively when this is discussed.

ACTIVITIES TO SUPPORT USING PUBLIC TRANSPORT AND/OR THE SCHOOL BUS

Activity 1 – Researching together

Parents would generally like to know what kind of situation their child will be experiencing, particularly where they have little or no prior knowledge of this. This activity involves a research task for parents and then practice with their kids.

Activity 1A – Parents

Look into transport options for getting your child to school. In some places the only option is the school bus, but in other places there are trains, buses or trams that your child could take to school instead. Public transport has the bonus that it is unlikely to include such a big concentration of kids from their school, giving fewer opportunities for bullying behaviour. However, there is the drawback that these modes of transport make lots of stops in addition to the one for your child's school, creating the possibility that they could get lost in thought and then travel three suburbs past their school after failing to recognise when to get off! Gather as much information as you can on the school bus and other transport options.

Activity 1B – Sharing findings

Now share with your child the information you have gathered. You may wish to let them decide whether or not to use the school bus, or you may want to guide them to one option or another based on what you have discovered. After going through the different options, ask your child if there is anything they are concerned about and/or would like to know.

If possible, have a trial run – or trial runs – of travelling to school with your child. You can do this during school holidays or at the start of term. Where possible, include your child in working out what needs to be put in place to support them in using the school bus or public transport to get to school.

Activity 2 – Taking the bus

If your child is a confident technology user and your local public transport system has an app, download this. If not, get a paper timetable and map and plan the journey with your child. Accompany them to the bus stop and remind them how to pay when they get on. Sit behind or in front of them and, if necessary, prompt them at the stop where they must get off. Repeat this as often as necessary until your child is confident. Then follow behind in the car for a couple of journeys. In some areas there are organisations that can do this with your child as part of their support plan.

Activity 3 – Changing buses, trams or trains

Once your child is confident with Activity 2 and can take a single bus (or tram or train) independently, then you can work with them on a more complicated journey in which they need to change buses or trams or trains. Again, you will probably need to accompany them initially. This is where apps can be really helpful as they can detail the journey and update it in real time.

DEATH OF A GRANDPARENT OR OTHER RELATIVE

Death is something that we all face. Young children may be largely oblivious to death, or, if they are aware of it, they may struggle to understand the magnitude of the event and the finality it involves. This is true for autistic and non-autistic children alike. Some young children don't know anyone who has died, which makes death all the more distant. Some may lose a grandparent, other relative or pet and experience grief.

One of the difficulties around death is that many adults also feel very uncomfortable thinking and talking about it. Without realising it, children may ask questions that make it all the more real and immediate to their parent. Questions around funeral customs, whether everyone dies or where the deceased person has 'gone' can be very confronting to a parent who is grieving themselves and who may struggle to determine an appropriate response to their child.

As previously mentioned, autistic children and young people may not know how to react to the death of a family member. They may be concerned that they might be doing their grieving 'wrong', and be more worried about that than their actual sense of loss. They may take a long time to start experiencing grief, which can make them seem unfeeling or detached when in fact they just need more time to process their grief. Autistic children are generally not callous or unfeeling and may actually be exceptionally emotionally affected but have alexithymia ('emotion blindness') and are unable to connect with their grief, or they may be terrified that people will judge them for doing the process of death and grief – which may seem very formalised – 'wrong'.

Autistic children may talk with peers or family members about death and the process of dying. They may seem very interested in it and might say things that upset or confront other children. This is often the result of them working through their understanding and their own grief. The emotions of others – and the expectation that there will be emotions from others – can be overwhelming for autistic children who are empaths. Their own grief mixes with experiencing the grief of family members almost through osmosis as empaths, which can be confusing and overwhelming. Autistic children may internalise grief and not respond in the expected way. Their grief may impact on their life and behaviour in the future, but they may in fact be unable to articulate what is going on. Some autistic children may seem more upset at the death of a pet than of a relative. This does not generally mean that they don't value the human inhabitants of their world. However, a pet often provides love and companionship for an autistic child every day, and many autistic people share a special bond with their pet. So, hypothetically, when Grandpa who lives two states away and who your child sees twice a year passes away it is understandable your child may be less upset than when their cat – who they confided with about difficulties they were having at school and who slept on their bed every night and gave the child affection and connection – dies.

If parents are not aware of these aspects of grief, their children's behaviour may be concerning. It is often the case of applying the lens of 'different not less' and working with children to get through the grief to a place of understanding and acceptance.

There are no real 'performance indicators' around grief. The process of grieving is different for each person – there isn't really a 'right' way of doing it. However, some signs that your child is managing their grief at the loss of a loved one include these:

- They are able to talk to you about their experience of grief, whatever that may be.

- They are aware to some extent of the impact of the death on their own life.

- They accept – possibly with some prompting and support – that their response to the death isn't 'wrong' and that everyone grieves in their own way.

STARTING A BANK ACCOUNT AND LEARNING TO MANAGE MONEY

Being able to manage money is a highly useful skill for independence and for life generally. Ideally, autistic children will grow up and get a job, although that may not be possible for some. Whether or not someone works, being able to budget and to understand how to manage financial matters is very important. Things like savings, budgeting, using credit cards, taking out loans and spending wisely form the basis of financial capability.

Acquiring financial capability is a valuable skill and supports independence. Not understanding how to manage money can have the opposite effect, fostering dependence and poor self-esteem. It is preferable for autistic young people to have developed their skills at managing money before they reach adulthood, not only because these are skills that they need but also because these skills, and the attitudes that go with them, tend to be easier to acquire at a younger age and are then easier to build and consolidate prior to reaching adulthood.

For autistic young people, some of the issues around managing money include:

- difficulty in saving or in seeing the point of saving

- a lack of understanding of the value of money

- for some children, a sense of entitlement and not understanding that not everyone's families are wealthy

- anxiety around having no money or – if they have savings – worrying that they will lose it all

- impulse spending

- difficulty in understanding the consequences of having no money

- difficulty with credit and loans, and not fully understanding how credit works.

Managing money successfully and learning lessons along the path to managing money can be great opportunities for your child in building self-esteem and a sense of pride in their skills. There are clear tangible results from managing money well. Things like opening a bank account or reaching savings goals can be a great motivator for your child. When teaching them about managing money, making the whole experience fun and engaging can help a lot. Money can be a rather a dry subject if not presented in an interesting way: if your child finds discussion of finances dry and boring, this will make it hard to instil in them the value of learning how to manage money.

If your child cannot recognise money, then this is the first thing to work on. Matching coins and notes with the concept of high and low value is really important. Autistic young adults may not understand that the £20 note is worth more than the £10 note, and may therefore struggle to manage money and be taken advantage of financially.

People have different temperaments in regard to money, though these can be influenced by family attitudes and spending/saving habits. Demonstrating the practice of saving money and talking about spending decisions with and in front of your children is very helpful.

Signs that your child is doing well at learning how to manage money include:

- They are interested in learning about managing money.

- They ask questions about money and budgeting.

- They have an increasing capacity to manage whatever funds they have (for example, their savings increase).

- They express interest in generating income.

ACTIVITIES AROUND MANAGING MONEY
Activity 1 – Savings and incentives

Opening a bank account is a great place to start your child on their journey to financial capability. They can set up a savings account – some banks have special programmes for children and young people.

Going into the bank can be viewed as an adventure and can make your child feel grown up, but it can also be anxiety-provoking. Prior to opening the account, discuss savings and the bank with your child. Ask your child to identify something they really want. (You may need to narrow this down to something they can afford after achieving what you think is a reasonable savings goal for them.) Tell your child that the savings account they will open will enable them to buy the thing they really want in a certain period of time. You can set a small reward at different points in the savings journey. You can have a little celebration at each milestone along the process. This activity will not only enable your child to learn how to save and to use a bank account, but should also make them identify saving money with enjoyment.

If and when they reach their savings goal and buy the thing they really want, you can mark the occasion with a celebration and talk to them about their next saving goal.

Activity 2 – Budgeting

Young people need to learn the importance of budgeting. Putting in place an understanding of how to manage money gives autistic young people a great start in terms of independent living and managing life as an adult. It also has value for children and teens in the here and now.

Instead of starting with a household budget, you can start with an activity budget. You can allocate money to your child for this activity.

- Decide on the amount – this can be as small or big as you choose.

- Decide on what the amount needs to cover – a trip or a meal or an activity, or some combination of these.

- With your child, look at different options for using that amount of money.

- Together decide on one of the options.

There are a large number of websites that can help with managing money: some examples are given below.

- https://www.moneysmart.gov.au/life-events-and-you/families/teaching-kids-about-money

- https://www.learningpotential.gov.au/learning-through-pocket-money

- https://www.moneyadviceservice.org.uk/en/articles/how-to-help-teenagers-manage-their-money

- https://bettermoneyhabits.bankofamerica.com/en/personal-banking/teaching-children-how-to-budget

Activity 3 – Budgeting for food and other necessary items

(If your child is not interested in food, this activity will not be a good starting place for budgeting, and you may instead start with Activity 4.)

Assign each family member a day of the week for planning a meal. Demonstrate how to plan and budget for a meal. Work with your child to plan a meal using a set budget – this could be a home-cooked meal or a ready-prepared meal from the supermarket, or a take-away meal.

If your child can do this easily, then you could increase the number of meals per week for which they are budgeting.

Activity 4 – Budgeting for non-necessary items

If you give your child pocket money, it is helpful to do this only if they contribute to the running of the household in some way. This contribution should be both age- and ability-appropriate.

Your child will need to learn how to budget for non-necessary items whilst prioritising things that they need. You can introduce the idea that they have to buy one or two things that they need with their pocket money, and they can then spend the rest on what they want. If your child is not able to recognise money or to understand the concept of value of money, this will need pre-teaching first.

CHAPTER 4

COMMON CHARACTERISTICS OF AUTISTIC YOUNG PEOPLE AGED 16–20 YEARS

WHAT IS LIFE LIKE FOR AUTISTIC TEENS AND YOUNG ADULTS?

Autistic teens – like any teens – are going through a period of change: physically, emotionally and socially. Being a teenager can be a time of discovery and growth, but it can also be filled with challenges and difficulties. Teenagers are going through physical changes related to puberty. In addition, they often experience emotional changes and growth in their level of maturity and understanding of people and the wider world. Working out their social groups and allegiances, their belonging and identity, are together an important focus in teenage years and motivate a lot of their behaviour and thinking.

The teen years are a critical time for the development of attitudes that young people will take into adulthood. The teen years are dreaded by many parents, and the fear of their children becoming 'terrible teens' is often realised, with anger and arguments and what is perceived as unpredictable behaviour, from the perspectives both of the teen and of their parent/s. The emotional impact of these changes for autistic teenagers is often huge, and meltdowns or shutdowns may temporarily increase. Unfortunately, mental health difficulties such as depression and anxiety disorders often have their onset in the teen years.

Teenagers are often maturing in their interests and understanding of the world. Autistic teenagers mature emotionally, cognitively and sexually at different rates from one another and from non-autistic peers. It can appear that autistic teenagers experience two periods of puberty: a *biological puberty* at the same time as their peers, and a *social/emotional puberty* at a later time. During biological puberty, the hormonal changes can affect mood, as well as driving the physical changes that transform young people into adults. Some autistics become sexually aware during biological puberty, whereas others only become sexually aware during their later social/emotional puberty.

Many autistic teenage girls seem to discover a strong social conscience, being very concerned by things like animal cruelty and human rights issues. These issues can become all-consuming if they are not managed and other activities or interests introduced. Some autistic teens also become addicted to online gaming, as this can offer a much more predictable and welcoming place than the real world.

The teen years can be a dangerous time for any teenager, but this phase of life may be more confusing for autistics than any other. While there tends to be a perception that modern life has many more negative influences on children than days gone by, it is more reasonable to think that the teen years have been potentially damaging for as long as humans have been around.

For autistic teens, there may be more profound difficulties in understanding consequences, in evaluating choices or the intentions of others, and in understanding or engaging in risky behaviour. Peers — autistic and non-autistic alike — may encourage unhelpful behaviour. Parents may intervene and be met with defiance as the teenager distances themselves from parental control. As children mature, the level of consequences and the impact from their behaviour tend to become more severe.

When I was about 14, I went to the school disco. I didn't really like it, so I just sat in a corner. Some other kids asked me to look after their drinks. They were nice to me, because I did this really well. They asked me to go to the scout disco too, and I looked after their drinks again. Then at the girl guide disco I got curious and drank some of their drinks. They tasted horrible, and I am not really sure what happened, but after that the boys at school said all kinds of horrible things about me, but confusingly they were always asking me out too. (Mia)

When I was 15, I suddenly found I had a huge social conscience and joined a protest group. Most of them were older than me and at university. They drank wine and smoked marijuana, so I started to do so with them. It seemed very grown up. At first the marijuana made me giggly and relaxed. I had never felt that way before and thought it was wonderful.

After a while I started to feel more interested in catching up with my protester friends just because it would involve smoking marijuana. On one occasion I had a really scary experience of being incredibly paranoid after smoking marijuana, and I thought that my friends from the protest group were going to attack me physically. It took me about a week to get over that. That experience sort of spelled the end of my drug use, and I haven't done it since. (Amelie)

WHAT DOES RESILIENCE LOOK LIKE AT THIS LIFE STAGE?

Resilience will look different for each person, but some general indicators that your teenager is building their resilience include:

- They have an ability, or a growing ability, to set their own boundaries – and to respect those of others.

- They have a growing ability to seek help, or to recognise and express that they need help.

- They have a growing ability to manage change or to be less anxious about or impacted by change.

- They have a positive, or increasingly positive, self-identity. The young person is able to express themselves with less or little concern about others' responses to them. They value themselves and who they are.

- They experience less anxiety about new experiences.

- Their self-confidence is growing or becoming more evident.

- They are willing and able to express themselves as 'different' and to take on their own identity. This can be evident through their clothes and their fashion sense, their interests and hobbies, their preferences for popular culture, and the friends they choose.

- They take pride in their actions and things that they make, write, play, and so on.

- They propose activities.

- They start to express a positive and realistic wish for more independence.

- They are increasingly willing and able to try new things and/or to take on new challenges.

- They demonstrate some positive self-esteem and self-worth and belief in the idea that they are a 'good' person.

- They have a growing ability to respond well to things over which they have no control.

- They demonstrate some self-awareness or growing self-awareness.

FORGING THEIR OWN IDENTITY

While parents can understandably find their teenage child's forays into independence frustrating and at times terrifying, some degree of experimentation and rebellion is important in order for a young person to develop their own distinct identity. The wish for more independence and autonomy is not confined to those autistic children who are verbally articulate. Teens who do not speak and/or who have high support needs go through the same sorts of life stages as others do. It is important to note, however, that not all autistic teenagers go through rebellion and a wish for more autonomy.

A well-known Australian clinical psychologist has suggested that there are two types of autistic teenage girls: those who are 'goody two shoes' and stay much as they were as children, and those who are 'terribly out of control' and experiment with drugs and sex and rebel all the time.[8] As autistic women, we would say that there is a more nuanced range of experiences for teenage autistic girls. However, it is true that a number of autistic girls do use drugs and alcohol as a tool enabling them to feel more comfortable and confident socially, which can lead to higher numbers of sexual encounters and safety issues.

One of the elements of forging their own identity is the need for teens to take risks or to challenge the boundaries set by parents, school and society. This can be incredibly worrying for parents, but to some extent it is a good idea to let go of a little control (depending on the activity, of course). There are varying degrees of risky behaviour. One of the issues

8   Professor Tony Atwood, Minds and Hearts Institute. https//mindsandhearts.net

facing autistic young people is that parents may be so concerned about potential damage or danger that they may deny their teenage child the opportunity to try out different things and forge their own unique identity. For some young people this will feel comfortable and safe, whereas for other young people this will prompt further rebellion.

It is understandable and advisable to have concerns around safety, but the whole concept of resilience stems from supporting your child in taking on incrementally more challenging tasks to build their confidence and mastery. A problem of this process during the teen years is that the consequences of a poor decision can be considerably more significant than when they were small children. Judgement is required in this space, and it is important for parents to weigh up the likely consequences of an error. If the expected result is unlikely to cause physical harm or psychological trauma, it might be time to let go of some control and of course to support your child in learning from the activity – regardless of the outcome. It is important to impart to your child some concept of the range of consequences attached to risky behaviour. For example, the magnitude of a young person trying alcohol at a party, while not ideal, is unlikely to result in death or injury unless they drink large amounts of alcohol. However, if the teen drinks alcohol at a party and then takes the family car while intoxicated and experiments with how fast it can go on the freeway, this clearly has the potential to result in death or serious injury of themselves and/or others, as well as serious consequences for these criminal actions.

Autistic young people who are 'black and white' thinkers can struggle to understand the notion of *rules* versus *consequences*. As children they may have strictly adhered to the rules, but when they are teenagers they realise that the rules can be broken. This is where it is important to teach consequences rather than just rules. In addition, many autistics will only respect rules that they can see as logical or sensible, or as being based in social justice. This can mean that they may follow rules that other teens don't, yet not follow group norms and rules, and this can alienate them from their peers.

While this book provides information about supporting the acquisition of resilience by your child, it is a fairly high-level framework. You are the expert on your child and your judgement is essential to support your child through the teen years. In deciding which activities you will allow and which you will not agree to, you may find it helpful to adopt a cost–benefit analysis approach. Consider the impact of a decision if it went wrong and weigh up the possible benefits of that activity in their life.

For example, if your child has started going out with someone, weigh up the benefits to them of experiencing a relationship and everything that goes with it, and the costs associated with a potentially messy break-up. You could consider the character and trustworthiness of the other young person and how those might be beneficial or detrimental to your child. You could write this down and then weigh up the potential costs and benefits and use that to inform whether you support the relationship or not. It is important to note that most teenagers, autistic or not, can be contrary – if you tell them that they *cannot* see someone whom they may have naturally lost interest in very quickly, they may fixate on seeing that person far more frequently.

BELONGING, FRIENDS AND PEER GROUPS

While friends and peers are an important consideration in any child's life, for teenagers, peer groups, friendships and belonging can become incredibly important. This is true for non-autistic and autistic young people alike. Even those autistic young people who do not seem to need a social network are often aware of social status and peer groups at school or in other settings. In the case of autistic children who have never had a friend, this may often not be through choice, and when they find a like-minded young person or child whose company they enjoy sharing, they will take on that friendship. For some young people, this translates into doing things so that others will 'like' them.

Social expectations among autistic and non-autistic teens are often quite different. Autistic children and young people usually communicate on one level, rather than using double entendres or hidden meanings. Autistic teens may retain their childhood interests, whereas their peers may have different and changing interests. In addition, autistic teens are for the most part upfront and honest, and still unaware of the important role that tact and other social norms play in adult interactions.

Autistic young people can mature later than their neurotypical peers in terms of their sexuality and their interest – or not – in sexual activity. They may reach physical puberty and sexual maturity, but the emotional side of sexuality often develops much later. When they interact with their non-autistic peers this difference can be very evident and can result in bullying and teasing. This difference does not mean that no autistic teens are interested in sex – far from it – but rather that they may need a few years to develop their understanding and interest in their sexuality.

One significant difficulty associated with this is that autistic young people may not understand that someone else is interested in or asking for sex. It can also make them a target for sexual predators, so teaching self-defence or protection is incredibly important for parents of autistic teens – both girls and boys.

Autistic people often form friendships with other autistic or neurodiverse people. People are all individuals, and autistic people do not always get along with all other autistic people. However, it seems that it is often easier for autistics to understand and be around other autistics. While introducing your child to another autistic child or young person does not necessarily mean that they will become best friends, it can be very helpful to introduce autistic teens to autistic peer groups or activities where other autistic teens are present.

> I was diagnosed with Asperger syndrome as an adult when I was 20. It took me many years to accept autism as part of me. Even when I did accept it, I didn't embrace it. It was like a guilty secret. I would only tell people I was really close with. I think I expected to be run out of town or something!
>
> Life went on, and I got more confident as somebody on the autism spectrum, but I didn't really feel part of a community. I hardly knew any other autistic people and most of them I didn't feel a strong connection with. A friend encouraged me to go along to an event for autistic women and girls. I didn't really want to go, but my friend was persistent. I am so glad I went to the event, because it was where I found my community, my 'tribe', as people say. It was a key moment for me, my autistic coming of age. I am now involved in a lot of online groups for autistic women. I am so happy when other people get their diagnosis, because it can open up that community for people who probably never felt genuinely included or accepted. (Yumi – 'Coming home')

Many large towns and cities have autistic youth groups that may be worth exploring with your preteen or teen. It can often take a number of visits before your child feels comfortable in the environment, and many more visits before they make friends. However, some autistic young people can feel at home straight away. If no autistic youth group exists where you live, you could be involved in setting up a monthly activity for families with autistic preteens or teens.

SIGNIFICANT CHANGES – MOVING TO FURTHER EDUCATION AND/OR WORK

There are a number of significant life events and changes that autistic teens will encounter. These may be similar life events for non-autistic teens, and will include things like finishing school, undertaking further education and joining the workforce. There are some changes that all young people experience and others that are more common for autistic or other neurodivergent young people. Transition points from education to further education and/or work can form an indicator of the young person's level of resilience and independence. The activities in this book are aimed at supporting your young adult in reaching their potential and managing those key transition points well. This does not mean that there is a set path or a set of achievements that will mean they have succeeded. Rather it is about supporting them in supporting themselves when they reach those points. There is no specific timeframe for achieving such milestones and it is neither a defeat nor a disaster if they don't, but it is a great aim for you and your child to work towards and one of the key reasons that supporting their resilience is important.

It is not helpful to view people who do not or cannot work or study as 'losers' at the game of life. For some people neither work or study is possible in the short or long term. If people cannot study or work, they haven't necessarily 'failed', and neither have their parents. However, study and employment can open the doors to independence and adulthood for many autistic people. If a person has the ability to work or study in whatever capacity, then they should be supported in being able to do so. Work and study can have a range of enormous benefits to autistic people. These include:

- a sense of being part of something bigger

- a sense of purpose

- a sense of pride in their ability

- exposure to new experiences and people

- being included in the 'adult' world

- income and with it financial independence

- pride in themselves

- a career path

- the ability to challenge ableist assumptions and put-downs related to non-participation

- the opportunity to be a role model for other autistic young people

- a sense of achievement.

So, if your child has the potential to do those things, then surely they should be supported in becoming resilient enough to take on these large challenges, rather than being denied the opportunities to try? If study or work are an option for them, it would be very sad for them to be unable to engage in them because they lack the resilience to take on these big challenges. One of the common difficulties we see with autistic young people is a lack of engagement in school or the wider community. This lack of engagement often results from a strong focus in society – at school and at home – on what the young person *can't* do rather than what they *can*, and an unwillingness by adults in their life to expose them to situations in which there is the potential to 'fail'. We are doing a disservice to autistic young people if we deny them the chance to take on such challenges. The purpose of this book is to help you do just the opposite – to prepare your child to take on difficulties and challenges and to build their resilience so they can live a fulfilled life.

GETTING A DIAGNOSIS IN EARLY ADULTHOOD

While many autistic children gain a diagnosis at an early age, some will be diagnosed as teens or young adults. This may mean that they have a much greater awareness of the process and of the views of other people about the autism spectrum.

Many parents report that they feel guilty for not getting their child assessed for autism earlier. This kind of guilt is unhelpful. There are any number of reasons that impact on the timeframe for getting a diagnosis for your child. It is not really the fault of parents, and the fact that they are getting a diagnosis *now* is positive. While a lot of emphasis is placed on the value of early intervention, a diagnosis at an older age is not necessarily a terrible thing. In fact, some forms of early intervention can in fact be detrimental to some autistic kids. These include the kinds of interventions that focus on changing behaviour that is not 'wrong' but that makes the autistic child look different from their peers (such as therapy that tries to force eye contact or to stop the child from stimming). As with anything in life, starting in the present and not regretting the past is a good philosophy. You can't change the past, but you can help to shape the future for your child.

Recent research has shown that some of the most positive 'early interventions' for young autistics revolve around good parenting that teaches new skills in the natural family context. The implication of this is that you may already have provided excellent early intervention supports for your child, even if your child had not been diagnosed at the time.

A teen or young adult who gains a diagnosis can respond in a number of ways. For some it is experienced as liberating and overwhelmingly positive. It explains where they 'fit' in the world and becomes an important part of their individual identity. For others it is a shock that more gradually turns into understanding and self-acceptance. For still others, it may take months or years to reconcile themselves to the diagnosis. For a variety of reasons, these young people are likely to be uncomfortable even thinking about autism, and they will probably not want to engage in the autistic community in any way and will find reasons for their differences that are anything other than autism. These responses are all valid. Gaining a diagnosis is often a significant event in a person's life. As the teen years tend to be the time for understanding and forging identity, an autism diagnosis at that time can be particularly influential.

When seeking an assessment for your teenager, it is important to answer any questions they have as best as you can, to present a view that autism is a difference rather than a tragedy, and to introduce them to some autistic role models (in books, movies, blogs, etc.). You can encourage them to find out about autism if they are interested. There are a lot of resources for autistic teens and young adults, some of which are listed in the Useful Resources section at the end of this book. Be aware that going through assessment can be a challenging and anxiety-provoking time for your child. Their outlook and behaviour in apparently unrelated areas may change. Talk to them about things such as what the diagnosis would mean to them, one way or the other; explain that there are many other autistic teens and adults in the world; find out what their concerns are; and let them know that autism has strengths and benefits that come with it, and that they will be the same person whether they get a diagnosis or not. You can reflect on the value of a diagnosis as providing access to an identity and peer group and the ability to access services such as assistance in school.

Autistic identity is a vital attribute for many autistic children, teens and adults. Identifying with the autistic peer group can be a significant positive for autistic teens and young people – and for adults too. Without a diagnosis, many autistic young people join any peer group that will have them in an effort to be socially accepted. Sometimes these peer groups are not supportive or helpful, and can even lead to problems like drug use and criminal activity, which your child may become involved in from a wish to be accepted by others. Even without these very damaging activities, joining a peer group that doesn't accept their interests and behaving in uncharacteristic ways in order to gain acceptance both tend to be detrimental to the autistic young person's sense of self-worth and self-identity.

Some autistic young people feel as though they have lost themselves in an effort to be accepted by others. In contrast, many autistic people who join autistic peer groups report a genuine sense of belonging and the ability to be themselves. While not all autistic people experience this, for many joining their fellow autistics is a liberating and empowering thing. In terms of identity, coming to terms with one that is genuine is usually far preferable to pretending to be someone they are not, simply in order to be accepted socially. For teenagers who are often desperate to be accepted by their peer group, meeting other autistic teens and adults can be a great way to develop and reinforce their identity in a positive and affirming way. This is not to say that the autistic peer group will always be accepting, nor that it will always be good to be part of that group, but such groups tend to be more positive and genuinely accepting.

> When I was first in a room with lots of other autistics, it was amazing, I could just be me, without any worrying about other people judging me or not accepting my stims. Even better, many shared my sense of humour! (Jake)

Some common challenges for young adults on the autism spectrum are discussed below.

SOCIAL INTERACTIONS

Autistic people can struggle to make and keep friends and to make social connections. They may be ostracised at school and, less often, in further education. To blame this on the apparently poor social skills of autistic young people can be unhelpful. Autistic young people often have very good social communication skills when interacting with other autistic people. From this the inference can be drawn that, rather than having essentially 'poor' social skills, autistic people struggle to communicate socially with non-autistic people. So rather than trying to 'fix' the social skills of autistic teens and young people, it is better to equip them with knowledge that will enable them to socialise more easily in the community and to understand the non-autistic world better.

FORGING THEIR OWN IDENTITY

The teen years are a pivotal time for establishing a person's identity, and this is often true for autistic teens too. Teens should be supported in discovering who they are and what they want in life. However, for some autistic teens the idea of deciding what they want to do in life is extremely anxiety-provoking, and they may express the idea that they never want to grow up and that they want to live at home forever.

> When I was 15, I didn't want to grow up, I hated the idea of having to decide what I wanted to do. What if I got it wrong and I didn't like it? My mum kept telling me that it was okay to change my mind as long as I did something, work or study. I have done lots of jobs, factory work, care work, being a teaching assistant. It has been good trying different things as I know what I like and don't like now. I moved out when I was 17, but only to go and live with [an]other family. Then when I was 20, I went flatting which was much easier than I thought it would be. My family gave me lots of support and helped me manage. I love online gaming, and my online friends helped too. (Sam)

Some of the issues around identity include the young person's autism – and, by association, their identity as an autistic person – being belittled, invalidated or ridiculed. Actually, learning to value and respect themselves as autistic is a key part of teen years, which can be severely damaged if all they are presented with is the apparent deficits around autism and if all the messaging they receive is in the negative.

BOUNDARIES AND LIMITS

As mentioned earlier in the book, boundaries and limits are essential in building independence and resilience in young people. While teens may push up against boundaries, this does not mean that their parent/s or educators should simply give in. The angst from a teen in response to an unpopular boundary being enforced is often very difficult to ignore, but it is almost certainly doing the young person a favour if you enforce it and demonstrate the value of boundaries and limits.

> My mum had really strict limits for me about what time I could stay out until. All my friends were allowed out much later. I had to get my friend's mum to call my mum if I was going to stay at my friend's house. I used to get so cross, but actually I know that Mum did this to help keep me safe. Some of the things other people did when they were out late at night and their parent had no idea where they were! I liked that my mum cared enough to want to know where I was and what I was doing. Also, if I didn't want to do something or go somewhere I just said my mum wouldn't let me and everyone accepted that. I knew that when other kids said they didn't want to they were pressured until they gave in and did it or people stopped talking to them. (Anna)

ACADEMIC PRESSURE

Academic pressure in the later years of high school and when starting further education can be a cause of significant stress and concern. While some autistic students blitz every exam and assignment, this is something of a stereotype and not true of many autistic students. Autistics who are perfectionists can find exams and assignments particularly stressful and struggle with accepting less than perfect grades/marks. Autistics who understand that you can resit failed exams and that many people fail things sometimes are less likely to get distressed by exams.

Academic pressures, combined with social anxiety, bullying, coming to terms with changes in puberty, working out their identity and all the other parts of teenage life, can often be overwhelming. Understanding what the young person is going through and providing support and perspective at this time is very important. Making the young person aware that their workload generally comes in peaks and troughs can also help. It can be useful to revisit why they need to do assignments and exams or work placements, as this can help autistic teens to accept the need to do something they are stressed about.

MANAGING THE TRANSITION TO ADULTHOOD

In the late teenage years children may start to see themselves as moving into adulthood and all that comes along with it. Autistic young people may be concerned about this for a number of reasons. These include anxiety around doing 'adult' things like driving or working and not feeling equipped to do these. Emergent sexuality and gender identity, combined with the knowledge that sexuality is often part of adulthood but not feeling ready for sexual activity and/or a partner, or feeling conflicted about these, can cause significant anxiety. The idea of becoming independent from parents and living independently can cause a lot of anxiety too. It is important to ensure young adults understand that the timings in their life should be set by them – if they are concerned that they are not ready to do 'adult' things right now, that is okay and such things can be postponed.

Interestingly, some autistic teens easily and successfully transition to independent life at age 16, 17 or 18. Many of these teens are highly resilient and are driven by a particular passion or interest to live, study or work in an area that means they need to leave home. Autistic young adults who are transitioning to group homes face the same challenges as their peers going flatting.

PROTECTIVE FACTORS AND RISK FACTORS FOR AUTISTIC YOUNG ADULTS

While there can be some significant risk factors around acquiring resilience for autistic young people, some protective factors can be encouraged or initiated. Resilience can be seen as a self-replicating skill, with greater proficiency promoting more resilience and greater independence. Resilience often promotes greater levels of self-confidence. In fact, skills like self-confidence, resilience, independence and self-esteem are often linked, so that an increase in one results in growth in the others.

While resilience is often a difficult skill for autistic young people to develop, it is crucial to promote it where possible, and supporting and encouraging protective factors is a great way to do this. Protective factors for resilience are often more intangible skills, attributes and experiences.

Some of the protective factors that can promote and strengthen resilience include the following.

Self-esteem

Self-esteem is a key element in building resilience. The concept of a 'place of safety' (discussed earlier in this book) is a way to build self-esteem through your child knowing they are loved, valued and supported. The strength of this foundation will impact on your child's self-esteem and through that help them build resilience. Even if teens are challenging their parents and making negative statements about them, if they started life with a place of safety this is likely to make an impact on their sense of self-worth in teenage years and to be a positive backdrop to their development, even though they may not be consciously aware of it.

A strong positive relationship with parents or other trusted adults

Children – and teenagers – tend to respond well to positive adult role models in their life, whether from early childhood or later years. An adult role model or mentor – either a parent or some other trusted adult friend or relative or activity leader – can really help autistic young people build their sense of self-worth, confidence and resilience. Such a role model can help the young person understand adulthood better and can help them see themselves in a positive light. Many autistic young people are bullied and/or face other traumas, and can feel very alone amongst their peers. An adult role model can demonstrate a number of positives: that childhood – and school – ends; that being 'different' can be a huge plus in adulthood; and there is value in being true to yourself. Autistic adult role models in particular can be incredibly valuable for an autistic teen or young adult. These might be friends or family members, but could also be drawn from autistic advocates the young person knows through social media, books, and the like.

Focus on strengths – by parents, supports and the young person

Two threats to resilience in young people are low self-esteem and a belief in their own incompetence. The kinds of negative messages about autism that can come from many quarters – even from family members and teachers – may eat away at their self-esteem. Understandably, an autistic young person who has heard their autism described in strongly negative terms and who has not been given any sense of pride or value as an autistic person may struggle to develop self-esteem and resilience. A positive counter to this is to focus on the strengths of the young person and of autistic people generally. This focus can come from parents and family and from school and support services. Autistic people and their families get a lot of messaging from a variety of quarters about how autism represents a series of deficits and negatives and that autistic people are incapable of doing the things that their peers might be doing. There is even messaging that autistic teens and young adults are a burden on their parents, and other very negative views. Being on the receiving end of such messages makes it hard for a young person to take on any challenges at all, let alone build their resilience. However, when parents, other family members, teachers and support workers challenge this 'deficits' view and instead talk about what the child can achieve and praise their good work, this serves as a strong counter to that negativity and can help the child build confidence and resilience.

Praise and positive reinforcement and recognition can be part of this challenge to 'deficits' thinking. If the entire discussion of a young person's capability is focused on what they *can't* do – even when somebody 'praises' them from the viewpoint of deficits (e.g. 'You didn't fail your math exam. Well done!') – this makes it more difficult to build confidence and to take on new challenges. Having the expectation that you will fail at everything is not a good way of building resilience! Alternatively praise for skills or achievements can be a useful protective factor for resilience. Understanding the young person's skills and strengths and interests is important in this area. For example, if you know enough about something your child is doing to realise they are doing well at it, it makes it easier to give genuine praise. Praise should be for genuine effort and skill, though. Autistic young people often pick up on 'fake' praise coming from a parent who does not really know what their child is doing, so sincerity is important.

> I liked making models, and when I was 14, I wanted to learn how to spot weld. My mum got me a small spot welder, and I taught myself. Mum was always really supportive and gave me useful feedback about how I was improving. I hated writing, and if I ever wrote, mum also praised that, even if it was a rude note, which she said was a great way of communicating my frustration with her! (Sam)

Positive peer relationships

Peer relationships are incredibly important when it comes to building resilience and self-confidence. The friends your autistic teen has can either promote or threaten their ability to build resilience and to take on challenges. Teenagers – including autistic teenagers – are influenced by a number of things. For many teens, the views of their friends or peers are exceptionally important. Teenagers tend to value the respect, approval and acceptance of their peers and their friends. While this is not always the case, it is very often a significant contributor to how they see themselves and relate to the world. If peers are focused on positive things and the friendship is meaningful and genuine, that is a great thing. However, sometimes teenagers form friendships with, or try to impress, peers who are doing negative and self-destructive things. An example of this is peer groups where the 'friends' engage in self-harming behaviours. Not engaging in self-injury is a reason for being ostracised from such a group, so the autistic young person may engage in self-injury in order to be accepted. This can have a whole range of negative consequences. For parents it can be very difficult to convince their teenage child to steer clear of negatively-focused friends. A lot of autistic children struggle to be accepted at school and will take any friendship that is offered. Supporting and promoting positive peer relationships and friendship is really important. More resilient children tend to be less prone to needing approval from peers at any cost. However, this doesn't help much when it has already got to the point of them being friends with peers whose opinions or behaviour are damaging.

Ways to set up positive interactions with peers are joining a group that is structured in a way that will set up positive interactions, such as martial arts groups, Navy Cadets, guides, scouts, groups doing Duke of Edinburgh Awards, Outward Bound courses, St John Cadets, and art or theatre groups. Autistic youth groups may also offer positive peer interactions. Online gaming can result in very real friendships, though parents need to be aware of what their teens are doing online and to teach them explicitly about cyber-safety.

My parents wanted me to get to meet some more people and maybe make some friends, so they asked me what I would like to do. I couldn't think of anything, so they gave me some choices. I joined the Navy Cadets, because I liked the idea of maybe being able to join the Navy when I was older. Even though I was a cadet for three years, I wouldn't want to join the Navy! I did learn how to go camping with everyone and do a whole lot of things. I liked it because they showed us what to do when they were telling us, and the leaders were really strict, so no-one was ever mean to anyone else. (David)

I joined an autistic theatre group. It was amazing, some of the people were really good and some of us were still learning about acting, but it was fun, and everyone accepted everyone else, no matter what. (Elsa)

NAVIGATING AVAILABLE SERVICES
Assessment

Depending on where you live, different kinds of providers will be required to complete the assessment that may allow you or your child to access funding for supports, whether these are for education, communication or similar. Check with your paediatrician, general practitioner or local autism organisation for relevant and up-to-date information around assessment processes and procedures.

Psychologists

Psychologists may offer support services to promote well-being and resilience. These are usually most effective if the psychologist has a good understanding of the autism spectrum and is comfortable and skilled at communicating in an autistic-friendly manner.

Psychologists use different therapy models to address psychological issues and promote mental health and well-being. Each individual will respond differently to the different models. No one therapy model is 'right' rather it is a question of finding the right fit for your child. It is important to find a therapist who gets along well with your teen, preferably with them feeling able to discuss things freely in the therapy setting.

You can ask on social media and in support groups for parents of autistic children and young people whether there are any psychologists who are recommended. If your child dislikes the therapist and the therapy sessions become a battleground, then rethink either the therapist themselves or the model used.

Psychiatrists

Psychiatrists too may provide services to promote well-being and resilience. They can also prescribe psychiatric medications, if these would be beneficial – this applies only to a very small number of autistic children and young people. Management of anxiety and/or depression, however, may be more effective with psychiatric supports in place. Some autistic young people will develop a mental health condition or illness that may need the services of psychiatrist to diagnose and treat, at least initially.

As with psychologists, it can be beneficial to consult friends and other parents about which psychiatrist/s they have found helpful with their own children.

Public health services

Public health services, including dieticians, counsellors, occupational therapists and exercise physiologists, may offer a range of support services for autistic children, young people, adults and/or their families.

Books and blogs

When reading books and blogs, it is important to ask whether or not they are accurate and useful. For example, if a blog is focusing on 'curing' autism, the supports suggested are not likely to be helpful or effective. There are some examples of helpful resources in the Useful Resources section at the back of this book.

Support groups (online and face-to-face) for parents and teens

Support groups can also vary in quality and in interaction style. Parent-run groups tend to have a different tone and focus compared with groups run by autistic adults. (Some are run by autistic adults who are parents to autistic children.) Groups run by autistic adults tend to use autistic communication styles: these are honest and to the point, and this can seem confronting to people who are not expecting this.

Respite services

To qualify for respite services, whether these are paid for or funded by your regional or national government, your child and family circumstances usually need to have been assessed by either psychiatric and/or social work professionals. In many countries there are daytime, brief, overnight and longer-term respite services. Autism-specific respite services are often over-subscribed with very long waiting lists, and it may be that your child will receive as good a service from a non-autism-specific service, depending on their needs, age, interests, and so on.

Making connections with other parents to share what works well along the journey of raising your child can be a great support. Some schools already have parent groups for parents of children with additional needs. If your child's school does not, you could ask for assistance to set one up.

Positive and negative service experiences

There are many, many service providers that parents of autistic teens and young adults can access. They range from the most supportive and encouraging provider to the one you visit once and never go back to again! Despite there being regulation for service providers in many countries, a lot of the quality element comes from the attitudes and ethos of the provider and individual staff members, which is harder to regulate. Remember that for most services you are not obliged to continue using them, even if they say that you are.

What makes a good service provider?

A good service provider is one that includes many or all of these attributes:

- You and your child are listened to.

- There is equal and respectful communication between you or your child and the service.

- The service and its staff have a good understanding of autism and treat your child as an individual.

- You and your child are shown trust.

- Administrative functions are consistent, open and accountable.

- Autism is viewed through the lens of positive attributes, not just all of the potential deficits.

- Any issues are addressed promptly.

- The service has an understanding of autism and of co-existing conditions.

- The service seeks and values your input as a parent and also your child's views.

- The service provider takes on board constructive commentary and criticism.

What makes a poor service provider?

A poor service provider includes some or all of these characteristics:

- You and your child are not listened to.

- You and your child are not treated with respect and dignity.

- The nature of the interactions between service staff and you and/or your child are punitive and blaming.

- Autism is mostly or only seen in terms of deficits.

- Your child is treated as if they were a 'burden' to you and/or society.

- The service has a lack of understanding of autism.

- Your child is not treated as an autistic individual but according to a broad stereotype of autism.

- Administrative functions at the service are unaccountable, secretive and inconsistent.

- The service responds defensively and/or aggressively to constructive criticism and feedback.

- You do not feel comfortable that your child is using this service.

BUILDING SELF-ADVOCACY SKILLS

Self-advocacy is a highly useful attribute for autistic young people – and for everyone else, for that matter. The skills around resilience discussed in this book will impact on self-advocacy. The ability to advocate for oneself comes from a place of self-confidence and self-esteem. To advocate for oneself requires the basic belief that one is worth advocating for. Self-advocacy, like resilience, is something that takes some time to develop and mature, but it will improve and grow each time you flex the 'self-advocacy muscle'.

Parents can instil and support their child's capacity to self-advocate. The messaging you give your child about their autism and their autistic identity from an early age influences their capacity to advocate for themselves as they grow older. For example, beware of negative messaging about being 'bossy' if a child, especially a girl, shows advocacy or leadership – this is one example of when you can instead *promote* these qualities, and this can start quite young. An example of self-advocacy is when an autistic teen is able to say, 'I need to wear my headphones, because I will be able to enjoy the movie then.'

Tell your child that they have the right to be treated with respect, and that if people violate that right then they are allowed to stand up for themselves, and indeed *should* do so – this too is a valuable aspect of supporting advocacy. Autistic adults often struggle even to see themselves of deserving respect after years of bullying, abuse and messaging that they shouldn't make a fuss. Self-advocacy skills can continue to be developed and grown over time. Knowing that it is not only okay to speak up, but that in doing so they may be supporting others who *cannot* speak up, is an important lesson.

Autistic teens need to understand their strengths and support needs in order to be able to ask for accommodations or support, which is a part of self-advocacy. Role-modelling and practising self-advocacy at home can help teens to develop this skill and be more confident in self-advocating in the wider community.

PROMOTING INDEPENDENCE AND SELF-RELIANCE

As children grow, the work of building resilience may start to come to fruition, but it may still need to be nurtured and promoted by parents and ideally also by other responsible adults in your child's life. There are a variety of helpful strategies in building on and consolidating resilience and independence in autistic teens and young adults. These include:

- *Working together on controlled challenges.* The kinds of incremental challenges you put in place for your child and teen to promote resilience can be adopted by the young person as they grow to adulthood. If they are open to this and able to do this, it can be a great idea to include them in setting and working through controlled challenges. This is likely to mean that the challenges they take on are more meaningful to them, which may make them more determined and willing to work through them. It can also get them thinking consciously about resilience and make them feel more 'adult' in taking responsibility for their own well-being.

- *Giving agency and empowerment.* Agency and empowerment are the keys to a person being engaged in what they are doing. 'Doing for' a young person can be unhelpful. Although younger children will need more guidance and control from parents, older teens and young adults are likely to want and seek out more independence and control over their own lives. Giving a young person agency for some of the decisions they take around resilience can actually result in them taking the lead, and this can have flow-on effects in the rest of their life. However, for some teens, that level of responsibility can result in significant anxiety and perfectionism, which may result in the opposite of what parents intend to happen, with the young person being unable to take on controlled challenges. As with most of the topics in this book, parents need to exercise their own good judgement. If more agency around decision-making is given, you can check in with your child to see how they are managing it. If it is in fact proving detrimental to take charge of their own controlled challenges, consider postponing or revising the process. Reassure your child that they haven't 'failed'.

- *Focus on independent living where possible.* Some autistic young people will not be able to live 'independently' in the traditional sense and will need support and care with activities of everyday life on an ongoing basis. This does not mean that they cannot be independent in some other ways. Independence is sometimes seen as a problematic concept, as in fact everyone – autistic and not – is *interdependent*. We all need others to support us in living our lives. The concept of 'independent living' is different for each individual, with some people being able to manage living alone or with their partner and others requiring practical support in the context of supported accommodation. The key to promoting resilience in living arrangements is that the young person has a say in what happens in that arrangement, and that they feel they are in charge or at least that they have the casting vote when decisions are made. In some supported housing options this will involve ensuring that staff and support workers listen to and are respectful of your child's wishes, and work with them to build agency and empowerment. It is important to note that people's requirements for care and support may change and fluctuate over time.

• *Building on existing strengths and experience.* The activities in this book and all the work you have done and are continuing to do for your autistic child in building their confidence and mastery and their level of resilience all feed into one another. Ideally, each experience, each success and each setback build the tapestry on which resilience is woven. The teen years are a critical time for adding to knowledge and understanding and forging an identity, but these lessons and experiences continue throughout your child's life. Establishing the basis for this resilience journey in childhood and adolescence may set your child up for a life in which they can take on challenges and build on past experiences to navigate the world with resilience and confidence.

CHAPTER 5

YOUNG AUTISTIC ADULTS AGED 16–20

Strategies and Activities Around Building Resilience

This chapter will focus on a range of life events and developmental milestones that autistic young adults aged from 16 to 20 years old are likely to experience. In each case it will include a description of the life event and the specific issues that might pose a challenge for young autistic adults. Each milestone will also include information on what a good outcome might look like, as well as activities and strategies parents can put in place to help their young adult child develop resilience and set the foundations for independence by successfully navigating through that life event.

The activities in this book may be of value to young adults of all cognitive abilities, including those who speak and those who use other communication methods. The activities may require some adaptation to be effective for your individual young adults. As with previous chapters, the activity outlines draw on the concept that 'Parents know their own children better than anyone else'. The activities and information in this book can be seen as a framework with which to understand and support your child into adulthood, rather than as a prescriptive programme that must be followed exactly.

BEING TOLD 'NO' BY PARENTS – TEENAGE WISHES FOR INDEPENDENCE

Teens and young adults often seek more autonomy from parents. This is also true of autistic teens, including those of all cognitive capabilities, whether they speak or use non-speech communication. This wish for greater autonomy is not necessarily a bad thing and often demonstrates healthy development and an emerging self-identity.

Even so, teenage wishes for more independence can be unpleasant and anxiety-provoking for parents, so it is something that needs to be understood and managed well. Even those teens who seem to be highly rebellious and combative often do not want a world with no boundaries, on either a conscious or an unconscious level. What you see might not actually be the same as the teenager's real intent.

Many parents feel powerless to assert a boundary for their teenager and are tempted just to give in to their demands to avoid another argument. However, teenage rebellion is often about the young person pushing limits in order to work out their position in the family and the world, so giving in every time there is an argument can be very damaging. The angst from a teen in response to an unpopular boundary being enforced is often very difficult to ignore, but you are almost certainly doing the young person a favour if you enforce the boundary and if you demonstrate the value of boundaries and limits.

As children grow older and move towards adulthood, the potential consequences of their mistakes and poor choices grow in magnitude. The consequences of poor judgement in teen and adult years can be more significant than errors made in childhood. There are a number of things going on in the teenage 'world' that autistic teens may engage in that can be harmful. These include sexual activity, availability of and access to alcohol and other drugs, and driving – things that most teens have on their 'radar'. However, autistic teens can struggle with being aware of consequences and may also want to be accepted by their peers. Bullies can prey on autistic teens, using the promise of friendship to lure them to engage in dangerous, embarrassing or illegal activities. Parents need to be aware of the potential for this. It is vital to maintain your relationship with your autistic teen as much as possible in order to help them understand the difference between situations that are okay and those that are not.

It is also important to be seen to be consistent in terms of messaging and discipline. Autistic teens are often highly attuned to inconsistency in messaging, and any inconsistency can result in them losing some trust in you. 'You told me to do this, but didn't you do it yourself – that isn't fair!' It is important not to set absolutes unless you can fulfil them as promised. It can be helpful if you use your actions to demonstrate ideas that some things are hard and fast, whereas others are a 'grey area'. This is particularly helpful for teens, as a lot of the decisions they need to make about appropriate behaviour and good choices are not 'black and white'. This is a common issue for autistic people *per se*. A 'black and white' approach is okay in some areas, but in situations where you need to make a less concrete set response, then the ability to be aware of and practise understanding of 'grey areas' can be very useful.

Signs that your child is doing well with understanding and responding to boundaries and limits:

- They eventually accept the boundary or limit, even if it takes them some time to do so.

- Their response to 'no' or a limit is not extreme, aggressive or self-destructive.

- If they have had an inappropriate reaction to a boundary, they understand after this has occurred that their behaviour was unhelpful, and use that understanding to inform future behaviour.

- They understand the sorts of consequences that may result from their decisions.

- They understand, on some level, the concept of 'grey areas', and can apply this or understand it when prompted.

ACTIVITIES AROUND BOUNDARIES AND AVAILABILITY
Activity 1 – Learning reasons for boundaries

Talk to your teen about choices and about the potential impacts of decisions. You could ask them to think about a decision they made that had a negative impact – although it might be worth ensuring they don't pick one that was traumatic and caused them ongoing angst. Ask them to identify some of the impacts of that poor choice, on themselves and on others.

Now identify something that is a poor choice they *haven't* made, but one that you think they *might* make. Talk about this activity. Ask them to imagine that you were in this situation yourself and made a poor decision. Ask your teen to identify some of the negative impacts of this choice might be if you – their parent – made it. Then ask them if they would be happy for you to carry out that action. You can use this as a basis of teaching consequences, and thus the reason you set boundaries.

Activity 2 – Ongoing open conversation

This activity involves advertising that you are available for your teen to ask or discuss anything. If you are constantly setting boundaries and saying 'No', you might appear to be in opposition to your child. Autistic teens may mistakenly view this as you not supporting or loving them. If your child is seeing you this way, it is important to reassert that you are on their side and support and care for them, even if you say 'No' a lot. You can set a time when you will be available. Make sure your teen knows that it will be only you and them there – and anyone else they themselves decide to invite. If your teen does not take you up on the offer of a conversation, periodically remind them that the offer is still open.

ATTENDING THE SCHOOL DANCE, FORMAL OR PROM

Towards the end of high school or secondary school, students often have the opportunity to attend school dances, 'formals' or proms. Autistic students have as much right to attend these events as anyone else does, and should your child wish to go this is not necessarily something to discourage or question.

However, there are elements of school dance events that can be very challenging for autistic young people. These include:

- *Sensory environment.* There may be loud music and other noise, smells of perfume or hair products, the itchy feel of ballgowns or tuxedos, and laser lights or strobe lights.

- *Proprioceptive issues.* Not being able to feel the distance between where other people end and you begin can be a definite challenge when dancing!

- *Not having a partner.* For these events there is usually an expectation that students will go with a partner of the opposite sex. Many autistic young people do not have or want a partner, so they may feel pressured into asking someone out. This can result in high anxiety, and also embarrassment and shame if one or more prospective partners say 'No'. If your child is not heterosexual, has a divergent gender or is questioning their gender and sexuality, a school dance may throw a lot of the concerns they may have into sharp relief. They may not know whether it is okay to bring a same-sex partner with them.

- *Formal dress.* The clothes for these events tend to be formal – ball dresses and tuxedos. This may cause anxiety if your child has never dressed that way before. Formal clothes can also be uncomfortable.

- *Anxiety about others' opinions.* Your teenager may worry about being dressed or acting in an 'appropriate way'. Autistic teens are often acutely aware that others perceive them as different. While it is hard to look too different visibly in a school uniform, choosing a formal outfit can have the added drama of the young person worrying that they will be attacked and ridiculed for 'getting it wrong' and not conforming to the fashion expected.

All of these factors can make autistic teens reluctant to attend a school dance. However, some teens see it as an important part of their move towards adulthood and independence. Some teens see the school dance as a way to take ownership of their apparent differences, and it becomes an outlet for self-advocacy, which is actually a great thing.

This is a situation where it is wise to be guided by your child's wishes as well as your own knowledge of them. How might the issues they are likely to encounter impact on them? How could you or they address these?

The school dance might be a very enjoyable and positive event, or it might compound issues around bullying and/or lead to unwanted sexual activity or other damaging experiences. The best thing is to equip your teen with the knowledge that they need so that their experience at the school dance can be positive and beneficial.

Ella is 16. At the end of the school year there was a formal dance for the students finishing Year 10. Ella wanted to go but was anxious about a number of things, including what to wear and who she would have as a partner. She had never been dancing before and was worried she would do it 'wrong' or trip over somebody and make them angry. Despite these things she was really keen to go and talked with her mum about overcoming these difficulties.

Ella's mum focused on the good things about the formal but also talked Ella through the potential difficulties. Because Ella had not been to a school dance before and was anxious, her mum told her she would be in café nearby when the dance was happening, so if Ella needed to leave or go home, she would be able to almost instantly – she just needed to message her mum. Ella ended up not going with a partner, as she didn't know anyone she wanted to take along, but her three friends and her went together.

Because her friends were there, and her mum was close by and because they had talked though any issues or concerns beforehand, Ella actually had a great time. She and her friends ended up dancing together, and they all enjoyed it. (Ella)

Signs that your child is doing well around attending school dances, formals and proms include:

- They are able to arrive at a decision as to why they do – or don't – want to attend.

- They have an understanding of what is likely to occur at the event and what they will do once they get there.

- After they have attended, they say that they enjoyed the event.

- They are not extremely anxious around preparations for the event, and whatever anxiety they do have is manageable.

- They are aware of potential issues and are able to manage these, either alone or with your assistance.

ACTIVITIES AROUND SCHOOL DANCES, FORMALS AND PROMS

Activity 1 – Anxiety, fantasy and reality

Talk to your child about whether or not they want to go to the school dance. Are they anxious about it? Can they pinpoint what they are anxious about? Are there people who are making them feel they shouldn't – or should – attend?

Work through their concerns and address anything you can. If your child states something that is highly likely *not* to occur, work through that too, explaining why it is unlikely. At this point you can prompt your child to explain, if they can, why it is unlikely. Use your judgement here, though, as some autistic young people have more capacity than others to work through the motivations of neurotypical people and reasons why things occur. If you are not clear about some of their thinking, you can prompt with questions.

The discussion can help inform your child's decision as to whether they wish to attend the dance or not, and it can also help to address their anxiety if they – and you – have decided that it is okay for them to go.

Activity 2 – Contingency planning

If your child decides they want to attend the school dance, then it is important that they are supported in doing so. It is likely to be more difficult for autistic and neurodiverse students to be comfortable and confident at a school dance, and it is likely that they will struggle socially and with new experiences. This does not mean that they have to, though. If your teen is worried about the school dance, then use this as an opportunity to build their resilience through supporting them to have a good time – or, if they *don't* have a good time, then to work out what the problems were and how to address them in the future.

This activity involves seeing the school dance as a project – with a timeline and deliverables or actions that need to be addressed to ensure that it goes well. What the 'deliverables' are will vary depending on the teen, but they are basically any blocks to your child having a good experience at the dance. They might be things like anxiety about finding a partner or worries about loud music or other sensory issues. In partnership with your child, work out a strategy or strategies to help address each of these concerns. Project deliverables might be things like going to the dance with friends rather than a partner, wearing noise-cancelling earphones if the music is too loud, taking dancing lessons or practising dancing with family members, and parents/s being available during the dance and providing an 'exit plan' in case things get too loud or stressful.

Activity 3 – Self-worth and standing out from the crowd

By the time they become teenagers, autistic young people often have a sense of their difference from others. While for some this can be experienced as a negative, others are proud to be who they are and are already doing some useful self-advocacy. This is largely a positive quality and something to encourage.

A school dance can be a great opportunity to promote the idea that a sense of difference does not mean *less*, and school dances are frequently used by students from diverse backgrounds as occasions for empowerment. If your child is in that space, that's great – but they still may require some support. This activity involves supporting your child in standing out from the crowd if they choose to, and to be there as their support person. Be very clear when speaking with them that your aim and intention is to be there for that at all times. Do not use ambiguous language or suggestion. Work through the outcome your child wants to achieve by 'standing out', what the implications of standing out might be, and talk with them about how you can work through difficulties with them, whatever may arise, and how their stand will help others.

PARTIES AND SOCIAL EVENTS

Parties are social activities that occur throughout a person's life. In childhood and primary school years, kids often have their first experience of parties at children's birthday parties. Some autistic children are more extroverted and enjoy these sorts of events, but for others they are very stressful and unpleasant. Even extroverted autistic kids can struggle with parties, and embarrassment and social anxiety can occur.

Social expectations, and notions of what is considered socially acceptable and what is not, tend to be heightened in the teen years. Parties can be a place where these notions of 'cool' and 'uncool' behaviour, as well as preferences in matters such as clothing and style, are very evident. For some autistic students, the combination of loud music and noises, lots of people in an unfamiliar setting, expectations of what is expected of them which they can't relate to and there being no 'script' for what will occur mean that teenage parties are off limits – even ones with responsible adult supervision and that are well planned. Some autistic teens simply do not attend parties. While there is nothing wrong with that in itself, if autistic teens want to attend a party with their peers they should be able to do this and should be supported in doing so. There can be some useful elements of resilience around social situations and more informal interactions, which may be gained by attending parties.

Some autistic young people are not invited to parties by their peers. This can quite understandably become a point of contention for them and make them feel isolated and excluded. If this happens with your child, the main task is to validate them and to support their sense of self-worth. Some parents have started campaigns to have people on social media send their autistic child cards for his or her birthday. Others organise parties with other family members and family friends. Both of these strategies can be very helpful in building up an autistic young person's self-worth.

Autistic young people do not need to attend teen parties to build their resilience, in fact, but these can offer a helpful way of building resilience around managing social situations.

Sometimes teens have parties that do not have adult supervision. At these events, teens may drink alcohol or use other drugs. Movies and TV tend not to help much, as they often depict parties like this as a sort of festival of independence or a rite of passage into adulthood. Students are depicted drinking alcohol and having sexual encounters – often for the first time. Autistic teens may emulate characters in movies whom they view as being socially acceptable and popular. They may use phrases they have heard in movies or on TV, or carry out actions they have seen, thinking that these seem cool and that their peers will be impressed by them copying their role models.

Here are some of the 'messages' in movies and on TV relating to parties, social events and school dances:

- Drinking excessive alcohol is fun.

- At the end of a school dance, people are supposed to have sex and lose their virginity.

- Sexual harassment is funny.

- You can have sex and there won't be any negative consequences (such as unwanted pregnancies, sexually transmitted diseases, or regret and shame).

- Nothing goes wrong at these parties – it is all harmless fun.

- It is exciting to be doing things without parental consent.

- There are no long-term consequences to any of the potentially risky behaviours in the movies.

In reality, alcohol consumption – especially for the first time – can have negative consequences ranging from the embarrassing to the criminal. It is important to separate the real world and the fictional world in your child's understanding of implications and risks.

Many autistic young people are scrupulously honest, but if they have been invited to an unsupervised party they may have been told or decided themselves not to share this with their parents. There is therefore a possibility that they will go without their parents being aware of this. However, some teens will tell their parents outright, or their actions and words will indicate to their parents that they intend to do something the parents may not approve of. This can be a very challenging situation as there are issues of trust and control involved. In this instance it is important to set and enforce boundaries, but also to take into consideration the forces acting when a teen wishes to attend such a party – pressure to be accepted by their peers, pressure to appear to be more like their peers, or wishing to have more independence and autonomy. These things are not excuses for making poor choices, but they are definitely mitigating factors.

When autistic teens attend a party – even one that they have really wanted to go to – they may in fact find it quite unpleasant due to sensory overload, social overload and anxiety around what to say in a conversation with someone you haven't met before.

As a parent it is important to know where to set and enforce boundaries around parties and social activities your child might want to take part in. Factors like potential risks around activities or peers, and the potential for your child to be taken advantage of in some way, must be balanced against the potential positives of the activity, including your child building friendships and social confidence, and resilience around social events.

It can be useful to develop a strategy around agreeing to social events that can help to inform your decision around a party or social event. Variables such as which young people will be attending (that you know of), what activity the young people will be engaging in, whether there is parental supervision and, if there is, whether the parents supervising will be supportive to your child if any issues arise are some questions to take into consideration.

It can be helpful to talk with your child about some of these considerations you are thinking about around parties. What do they need to know in order to stay safe? If you explain this, then even if they attend an event that has risky behaviour such as drinking alcohol or sexual activity, they have some knowledge and some strategies to deal with the situation in your absence. Examples of things about parties that your child could benefit from knowing include:

- that it is okay to *not* do something another partygoer asks or tells you to do

- that it is okay to leave early – at any time

- that it is okay to use headphones and other strategies for addressing sensory issues if you need to

- whom to contact if something goes wrong (emergency contacts)

- that each person has the right to decide on what sexual or other physical contact they have, and to tell another person 'No'

- what sexual activity – even if consensual – can lead to (e.g. pregnancy, sexually transmitted infections, shame or regret by self or others)

- the effects of drinking alcohol, particularly to excess

- what illicit drugs look like and some of their impacts, particularly on mental health.

For autistic teens, parties can be a great introduction to socialising with their peers, but they can also come with some significant risks and challenges which might result in your child struggling more. Use your veto and set boundaries if you are concerned about an event, and similarly promote a party if you think it will be a supportive place for your child. Some autistic children never attend a teenage party and others attend lots of them. There isn't a right or wrong with this, but it is helpful to be conscious of the issues and risks.

Signs that your child is doing well with parties include:

- Their anxiety does not stop them from accepting invitations to social events and parties.

- They understand and exercise some judgement around social events that are likely to be harmful.

- Parties are a mostly positive experience for them and result in their consolidating or making friendships.

- If they do not wish to attend, they are able to express that to their parent/s and to the person who invited them.

- They know clearly or with increasing clarity which parties, if any, they want to attend.

- They can raise with their parents any concerns they have around social events and parties.

- They have a plan for what to do if anything goes wrong at a party.

ACTIVITIES AROUND PARTIES

Activity 1 – Research project

Uncertainty around an outcome or situation can drive anxiety for autistic people. An invitation to a party might be both exciting and validating, yet also result in extreme anxiety. Often the anxiety is around protocols and social 'norms'. Even autistic adults can struggle with this. Things like the recommended dress code for an adult party can throw autistic adults into a spin. (What does 'cocktail attire' mean?) These anxieties can be heightened for young people. What if they dress 'wrong'? While in fact non-autistic people tend either to know this intuitively or to find it of little importance, dress codes and dance steps can cause high levels of stress for autistic young people.

This activity is of value when your child is anxious about 'formal' themes and logistical elements of a party they are invited to. It involves encouraging your child to do some desktop research about the different formal elements of parties, and those relating to the one they are invited to. They can report back and discuss their findings with you. It helps if you also introduce into the discussion a little perspective and discuss the relative importance of these elements. This can support your child in attending an event they might otherwise not have gone to, and to manage anxiety better when they *do* attend, building confidence for other social events in the future.

Activity 2 – Host your own party

This activity involves encouraging your child to host their own party. If your child is interested in attending a party but anxious about socialising with school colleagues, at their own party they can invite anyone they like – friends, family members, their pets. Work with them to develop the guest list – which may be one or more invitees. Ask your child to choose the music and a theme (if there is one). Then support your child in planning and putting on the party. As it is being driven by them, it is likely to be a more supportive first step into parties. If hosting the party allows your child to build their confidence to attend the party of a friend, or if it just means they want to have more parties that they organise themselves, then both of these outcomes are positive and will support resilience and self-esteem.

Activity 3 – Practise party conversations

This activity can be of use when your child has agreed to attend a party with a friend or friends, and when they have not attended a similar event before and are concerned about what might happen at the party, particularly around socialising with non-autistic partygoers. It can be hard for autistic people in an unfamiliar social setting or environment to work out things like how to initiate conversations and how to talk to more than one person at a time. This can compound their anxiety in an unfamiliar setting.

This activity involves a role-play with your child in which you act out with them some of the dynamics involved in conversations. You will need at least two or three people other than your child. Support your child with things like 'breaking into' conversations and talking to two or more people at once. Avoid trying to make them seem less 'autistic' or less like themselves as this will if anything dent their social confidence. They were invited to the party as themselves, so there is no value in trying to make them less who they are. The role-play is intended to help them feel confident in a different social setting, not to hide who they are. This activity can be an ongoing one as they build their confidence in social settings.

DECISIONS ABOUT ALCOHOL AND OTHER DRUGS

It has been said that autistic young people are either very well-behaved and compliant or the opposite of that – that they take risks and try everything, even things which can be dangerous. Some autistic teens have no interest in trying alcohol or other drugs, but many will do so, for a variety of different reasons.

There are a lot of myths about drug use – that someone can become addicted the first time they try a drug; that everyone who uses illicit drugs is homeless, unemployed or a criminal; or that some drugs are 'harmless'.

In reality, most drugs are *psychologically* addictive rather than *physiologically* addictive, meaning that if a person is in a positive place in their mind, where they do not need a 'crutch' to mask their pain, then it is highly unlikely they will become addicted to anything. Addiction is usually born out of difficult experiences and a wish to numb the pain.

One of the issues parents face is the difference in knowledge between them and their child in understanding the risks and consequences of alcohol and other drugs. This is true for most teens and young people, but for autistic teens it can be heightened. Many autistic people have alexithymia (or 'emotion blindness'), which means they cannot connect with their emotions a lot of the time. When talking about risks and consequences with young people who do *not* have alexithymia, the young person's emotional responses can be used to build their understanding of consequences, and what happens if risks eventuate and result in injury to the young person or to friends who are engaged in the same activity. With autistic young people who cannot access their emotions, however, this strategy tends to be a lot less effective as they may not be able to call on their memory of those emotions from the past. In this situation, using a more practical or concrete example can help, and then working through a list of the potential consequences to the young person and explaining what each consequence would look like. For example, 'You might go to jail' might not evoke a lot of responses, if that is beyond the young person's experience. Instead, relating it back to their interests and their daily life in practical ways is often a better approach. An example would be: 'You might go to jail, and then you wouldn't be able to talk to your family or your cat, and you wouldn't be allowed to have your phone or iPad…' (etc.).

A lot of teens experiment with drugs and/or alcohol, with different effects. This is certainly not ideal, and autistic teens and young adults can be susceptible to using alcohol and other drugs in a risky manner. Some of the reasons why autistic people might be more vulnerable to damaging drug or alcohol use include:

- *Trauma or anxiety.* They may have experienced trauma or have high anxiety. Alcohol and drugs usually produce a sense of euphoria and, while they are under the influence, enable people to feel 'better'.

- *Predictable feelings.* The effects of drugs or alcohol are fairly consistent for each individual who uses them. If you get drunk, you know how you will feel – you will feel drunk. Predictability around their inner world can be very attractive for autistic people who may struggle to manage emotions.

- *Seeking acceptance.* In order to be popular or socially accepted, autistic young people may wish to be part of a peer group that uses drugs or alcohol, and group members may pressure the autistic young person to use drugs or alcohol as well. Even if the young person doesn't enjoy the sensation of being under the influence, the need for social acceptance can outweigh any concern around negative consequences.

- *Cultivating a persona.* Some autistic young people develop a persona of being a 'bad boy' or 'bad girl'. This can be a means to mask others' perception of their being a 'nerdy' person, which is often compounded by bullying. They might get heavily involved in drug and alcohol use, sexual activity and criminal acts, in order to convince those around them that they are rebellious and independent from their parents and society. The solution to this often centres around building self-esteem, but this can take some time and understandably it can be harrowing for parents to see their child go through this. Strict discipline can backfire in this situation.

- *Reduced social inhibitions.* Some autistic people find that being drunk or high around others who are drunk or high enables them to socialise and not be seen as odd or feel isolated. When people are drunk or high, they tend to lose their social inhibitions, and this can be attractive to some autistic young people because it is easier for them to socialise with other people who are also intoxicated. They can experience social acceptance from neurotypical people where they might not in other circumstances.

Autistic people can be susceptible to some consequences of drug and alcohol use. Autistic young people are already more likely to be attacked by predators, but when they are high or drunk they can be at greater risk of unwanted attention. While this behaviour is entirely the fault of the predator, even so self-protection is vital. Some autistic people are very sensitive to drugs and either take a lot more or a lot less than others do to get the same effect.

For parents it can be extremely stressful to see their child doing things that potentially put them at risk. It can be difficult to know how to address this issue. For some young people discipline and 'laying down the law' can be effective, but for others this approach can be unhelpful and may drive the young person to more extreme behaviour. It is important to set a clear boundary and to enforce it. If the boundary around the behaviour is fluid and changeable – particularly if it changes when the young person pushes it – then it is likely not to work.

As much as possible, it is important to know the reason behind the young person trying drugs or alcohol: this should drive the response from parents. Below are some exercises that will help you understand the reasons for – and identify useful responses to – your child trying drugs or alcohol.

One issue for autistic people is the notion of 'grey areas'. Autistic people are often 'black and white' thinkers who focus more on the rules than on the ethics that might form the basis for those rules. They can be sticklers for the rules. Parents can experience this as a positive if they feel confident that their autistic child will not drink alcohol or try drugs because it is 'against the rules' and as such is 'wrong'.

The problem with this can arise when the child's or young person's view of the rules, or the predictability of their world, is challenged. This can be due to the basis of their life changing (e.g. separation of parents, a traumatic event such as sexual or other assault, or the real or perceived betrayal of a friend or peer group). It can also occur if a rule is broken but the consequences are neutral or appear to be positive. Being rules-focused can in fact be a concern in these situations, as new, damaging rules can replace the old ones. Teaching autistic young people about the ethics that underpin the rules (for example, the just laws of the country) can help with this. This 'rules' focus can be something that drives the kind of apparently inconsistent changes an autistic teen or young person can go through.

'Grey areas' can be difficult for many autistic people to comprehend. For many, something is either allowable or it is not allowable. Others will want to know the rationale for apparently everything, including why something is allowed and something else is not allowed. They can struggle to follow rules that they see as unfair or inconsistent. For young people whose thinking is like this, saying 'You aren't allowed to drink any alcohol until you are of age' may be ineffective as the rule might be questioned. Instead, it is best to explain the potential consequences of excessive drinking or the impact of alcohol on developing brains – these facts give some context when instructing a young person to avoid alcohol and illicit drugs. Some autistic young people, though, are more focused on things being right or wrong according to the rules. With young people who view things through that lens, it can be more helpful to set rules and say, 'You are not allowed to drink any alcohol until you are of age' or 'It is a criminal offence to use illicit drugs, so don't use them'. Young people are all different, so this advice is guidance to be taken on board and considered in the light of your own understanding of your child.

EXERCISES AROUND THE EXPERIENCE OF DRUGS AND ALCOHOL

These exercises provide examples of autistic young people who, for different reasons, have had difficulties with drugs and alcohol. Each scenario has questions at the end which are designed to build understanding of choices around drugs and alcohol, and to demonstrate some of the things parents need to consider.

Exercise 1 – Lee

Lee is an autistic 17-year-old young woman. Lee has struggled to make friends all through school. She was very anxious and embarrassed around other people her own age. She has some friends who are adults and is close with her parents, but until recently has had no friends at school.

About two months ago Lee told her parents that she had a friend in her year at school. She was really happy, as were her parents. After a while, though, Lee seemed quite distant. One of her teachers called Lee's parents because she had failed an assignment and missed several classes, which was totally out of character. Recently Lee came home from school an hour late and had her phone turned off. When she did get home, her mum smelled alcohol on her breath. Her parents were really worried, and her mum sat down with Lee the next day to ask what was going on. Lee very honestly told her mum that her friend liked to drink alcohol, and when Lee drank she felt relaxed, and she had never felt like that before, and it was wonderful.

Questions

- What do you think might have been the causes of Lee's drinking?

- Was alcohol, the new friend or something else responsible for Lee's changed attitude and behaviour?

- How would you approach addressing the issue? Would you focus on the friendship or something else?

Exercise 2 – Denny

Denny is an autistic 18-year-old young man. When he was younger, he was a 'straight A' student, who loved anything to do with physics or engineering and was very keen on online gaming. Denny was the quintessential autistic 'little professor'. He had a vast general knowledge and would talk to anyone about his passionate interests. Denny was singled out by bullies right through school. He was physically and verbally attacked. Denny was cyber-bullied as well. His parents did everything they could, talking to the school and to other parents, but eventually, when he was 13, they homeschooled Denny. He was really relieved to be away from the school environment, and his mood improved almost instantly after starting homeschooling. Everything was going well – but then, apparently out of the blue, Denny started to disengage from his family.

Denny had joined a peer group of mostly young men of his age. This group used drugs and alcohol and engaged in some petty criminal behaviour – graffiti, mostly. His parents asked Denny what was happening, but he usually got angry and yelled at them. He was most upset if they reminded him of what he was like when he was younger: it was as if he wanted to forget the past.

Questions

- What might some of the reasons be that Denny is so rebellious?

- Why do you think Denny used drugs and alcohol?

- Can you think of any ways to 'reach' Denny?

Exercise 3 – Josh

Josh is a 16-year-old autistic young man. Josh was invited to a party by some people at school whom he didn't know well. When he got to the party, there was a lot of alcohol and people were drinking. Josh hadn't really been around alcohol much. He knew it was illegal for him to drink and he didn't really want to have any, but the other people at the party told him to drink some, so he did. At first Josh felt relaxed and talked to people he wouldn't normally talk to. He laughed a lot, and it was fun, but then he started feeling very heavy and tired and nauseous. He also sensed that others at the party were making fun of him, but he couldn't tell for sure. They kept telling him to drink more. Josh went outside to feel the cool breeze on his face. He lay on the grass and slept. When he awoke, it was dark. He felt really sick and had a headache. He needed to call his mum to pick him up, but he was worried that he had done the wrong thing and it was really late so he walked home, which took over half an hour in the dark.

A few weeks after the party Josh told his mum what had happened as he doesn't like to keep secrets or lie. His mum told him it was okay, and it was the other kids' fault, but Josh was really upset and felt guilty.

Questions

- How should Josh's mum approach this incident, and what messaging should she give to Josh?

- How could Josh be supported in understanding that even though he 'broke the rules', in this instance it was not so much his 'fault'?

- What conversation needs to happen around 'rules' versus 'ethics' to help address Josh's guilt?

MAKING INDEPENDENT DECISIONS

The capacity to make independent decisions is an important element of being resilient and independent. It is important to note that the meaning of 'independence' varies for each person. Independence certainly does not mean that a person is able to do everything with no assistance. Independence is more about a person's capacity to access and utilise appropriate supports to manage their life well. Independence may look different for people with high support needs and those who need less support: independence is specific to each individual. There is no ideal of independence. Thus there is a goal for independence, but it is specific to each person and their needs and circumstances.

The capacity to make independent decisions also varies according to the individual. Some autistic teens and young people will really struggle with independent decision-making, while others are able to take it on relatively easily. The difference between those poles can be influenced by the level of resilience and independence the young person already has, but the process of building decision-making confidence and competence can, in turn, influence their resilience and independence. This can be very difficult if young people have not been allowed or able to make decisions around their life in the past. Like resilience, it is something that cannot be acquired quickly.

The activity of making independent decisions involves a range of different choices, from what movie to watch to which university courses to apply for on leaving school. Some decisions have greater consequences and impact than others. For some autistic young people, even apparently minor decisions can cause high anxiety. In this instance it can help to apply the principles of controlled challenges, the place of safety and failing successfully, as outlined in this book, to the practice of decision-making. Start small, with decisions such as 'What movie shall we watch?' and 'Which restaurant should we eat at?' Support the young person as they build their confidence around decisions; and if they make a poor decision, try and use the experience to build understanding and knowledge to assist them in making decisions in the future.

The ability to make decisions for oneself is a driving force for independence. Even decisions that seem unimportant can support an autistic young person in empowering themselves and building their confidence. It can be very helpful to let go of a little control on minor things to enable your child to build their confidence around making decisions.

When a young person starts making decisions independently, however, it can be difficult for parents. Parents can experience anxiety and concern for their child as they grow older – the older a child gets, the larger the consequences tend to be of any mistakes or poor decisions they make. But it is essential to support your child into independence as much as you can. Parents of autistic children can be particularly protective – and often for good reason – but it is important to start letting go of some control as they move towards adulthood. Growing independence can be as much a test of resilience for parents as for their kids! This gradual parental letting go involves a process similar to that for the controlled challenges used to support resilience, as outlined in this book.

Building independence can be a risky business for autistic young people. It can backfire – a decision might have a negative consequence, or the young person may lack the confidence to take the decision. At times, building independent decision-making can be a 'two steps forward, one step back' kind of situation. Even though parents let go of some control, this process is not irreversible – they may need to step in again for a while and then, when things are going better, let go of some control once again.

Signs that your child is doing well with making independent decisions include:

- They have some understanding of the need to move toward independence and the need to start making independent decisions.

- They are able to make some decisions appropriate to them and their circumstances.

- They are not extremely anxious, or are decreasingly anxious, at the prospect of making decisions.

- They are positive and keen to take on more decision-making responsibility.

- If there is a setback, this does not stop them from continuing to work towards independent decision-making.

- They make some decisions for themselves.

- They make good decisions.

- They learn from poor decisions and mistakes.

ACTIVITIES AROUND RESPONSIBILITY AND DECISION-MAKING

Activity 1 – Taking on responsibility

With or without encouragement from you, your teen takes on responsibility for something they enjoy or are interested in. Let them know that this is *their* task – that you are there for support if needed, but the main responsibility is theirs. You can help your teen set goals and milestones. This can be done around a number of different tasks to build confidence. Use your parental judgement, but try to step back as much as possible and occupy more of a consultant role.

Activity 2 – Researching decisions

Work with your teen to determine an activity they are interested in. Talk to them about the decision and what they know about it. Set them a research project of finding out the information they need to make the decision, tailoring the exercise to their capability and interests. Give support if needed, but try to let it be 'their project'. Depending on how your child learns and works, you could set a deadline to report back or have the reporting happen during the project in an incremental manner.

When the research is complete, have a discussion with your child to see if they have arrived at a decision. Work with them to make the decision and support them in following it through. They may come up with a decision that isn't ideal – it may open them to risk, for example, or be likely to lead them into a difficult, traumatic or dangerous situation. However, decision-making is also about being able to revise and reconsider your decisions, so in this instance help them work out what the consequences of the decision they reached might be and support them in making a more positive decision.

THINKING ABOUT DRIVING AND LEARNING TO DRIVE

There is a common stereotype that autistic people cannot or should not drive. In fact, many autistic people do drive. As with anyone else, driving proficiency varies across different autistic individuals. Autism is not necessarily a factor in a person's ability to drive well or poorly. While there are some issues that autistic people may face that might impact in driving – such as visual and other sensory issues, hyper-focus or anxiety – there is no reason why autistic young people should not be given the opportunity to learn to drive, although some aspects may require additional attention when they are learning.

In many countries, gaining a driving licence is seen as a rite of passage. Having a licence signifies a range of perceived positive qualities, such as independence, responsibility and adulthood. In some places not being able to drive can impact on independence – some places and activities might otherwise be inaccessible, due to inadequate public transport or the costs associated with taxis and other car for hire arrangements. This is particularly the case in rural and remote areas.

Driving comes with a lot of responsibility. Car accidents may result not only in injury or death, but also in criminal charges. The range of rules around being on the road can be overwhelming for autistic new drivers, and anxiety around these issues can be overwhelming and even harmful to mental health and well-being. The large amount of responsibility associated with driving can put off some autistic people. Conversely, other autistic people might pride themselves on being good and responsible drivers. They may be highly conscientious and aware of their responsibilities.

Some autistic young people and adults will never drive, for a variety of reasons including anxiety, sight issues (e.g. poor depth perception) and issues with coordination and focus. It is important to note that for some autistic young people, driving is not something they will have any interest in doing. It can be difficult to know where the line is between investigating the possibility that they might learn to drive and pressuring them to do something they do not wish to, and which might cause overwhelming anxiety. Someone who is strongly averse to learning to drive as a teen or young adult may revisit the possibility when they are a little older. It is important not to invalidate or dismiss a young person's decision to drive or not to drive, but to set out the pros and cons and to work through and resolve any questions or concerns they have.

In some countries there are driving instructors who work specifically with learner drivers who have a disability or autism. This can be a good option for young people who are very anxious about the possibility of learning to drive, or for those who might be a little too confident and not fully realise their responsibilities as a driver.

If an autistic young person expresses an interest in learning to drive, then preparing them is crucial, and not only for the test. You need to explain what their responsibilities as a driver will mean, and to convey the idea that driving involves not only the practical aspects of controlling the car but also knowing how to be a safe and respectful road user. When you talk to them about understanding their responsibilities as a driver, be careful not to terrify them and put them off, but make them aware that there can be serious consequences of driving carelessly, recklessly or without thinking.

Understanding the road rules is vital for any driver, but autistic drivers may benefit in addition from unpacking the implications of the road rules and the reasoning behind them, and may also benefit from knowing that driving is a form of interpersonal communication between all of the people using the road. 'Defensive driving' principles can help the young person to be aware that even if they themselves are obeying the rules and driving well, other drivers might not be.

It is also important to be aware of insurance coverage, legal responsibilities if involved in an accident, and how to respond to police if stopped or at an accident. Autistic people – particularly young men – can be perceived by police officers as non-compliant or under the influence of alcohol or other drugs, even if they aren't. Police officers often meet other people who *are* being 'smart' or non-compliant, which means that an autistic person's communication may be misunderstood by officers as disrespectful or deliberately cocky. The potential for very negative consequences to this is all too obvious, and the response if the police arrest or challenge an autistic driver can escalate things when all that was really happening was a misunderstanding. It can be helpful if autistic people carry a card or have a statement prepared in case they are stopped by the police: this can state that they are autistic and what that means for the person.

Signs that your child is doing well in considering learning to drive include:

- They are realistic about the process of learning to drive.

- They have an understanding of what their responsibilities would be as a driver.

- They show an interest in investigating the pros and cons of learning to drive.

- They are enthusiastic about learning.

- If they are anxious about the prospect of driving, they are able to consider the possibility and respond to efforts to build their confidence.

- If they do not want to drive, they are clear about their reasons and, with some prompting if ncessary, can explain their concerns to you or to others directly.

- They have a plan of action around learning to drive (e.g. 'I will start learning after school finishes, so that I can focus on driving and not be distracted by my schoolwork').

ACTIVITIES AROUND DRIVING

Activity 1 – Lessons to prepare for driving lessons

If your teen expresses an interest in learning how to drive, take them for a series of drives. During each trip, explain to them *one* element of driving, such as using your mirrors. Repeat this for different elements of driving. For some teens this can alleviate some stress around the technical process of driving a car. Some teens will learn more quickly while others will be slower; and they may have more or less confidence, depending on their individual circumstances, character and personality.

This activity is about reducing anxiety around driving, and in particular the technical aspects. You should be guided by your child's own circumstances. Some may pick up skills – and the confidence to put them into practice during driving lessons – more quickly than other young adults.

Activity 2 – Motoring mentor

If possible, invite an adult autistic person who has driven for some time to talk to your teen about their experiences of learning to drive and driving. If this person is somebody your teen already knows and respects, this is likely to make this activity more meaningful and valuable for them.

Autistic young people are often told that they cannot drive or that if they did they would be terrible at it. In fact, many autistic people are proficient and confident drivers. If your child picks up on the stereotype that autistic people are poor drivers, this is very likely to sap their confidence and put them off even trying. Having an autistic adult introduce different thinking to your child about driving can be really helpful.

Activity 3 – Driving skills

If your teen is anxious about driving but wants to learn, you can introduce them first to the supplementary aspects of driving. Show them how to pump petrol/gas. While the car is stationary, show them the different controls. Encourage them to sit in the driver's seat and to work out where each control is and what it does. For someone who is anxious about the process of driving and their ability to manage the mechanical part of driving, this may help settle some of their concerns.

Activity 4 – Front-seat driver

While part of driving involves working the mechanics and controls of the car, a lot of driving is about using the road safely. Even if your teen is going to become a great driver in terms of technical control, they need to be aware also that driving is in some sense a social interaction between them and other drivers on the road.

Driving – at least when someone first learns – involves a level of awareness that can be quite different from the awareness needed in other situations. You need to control the car and to be aware of what is going on regarding your speed, how much fuel you have and so on, but you also need to interact safely with the other road users and to pick up cues from street signs and signals from other drivers. For autistic people it can be challenging to be aware of all those different things at the same time. This activity involves you explaining to your teen the things they need to look out for while driving, in addition to managing the car itself. Each time you go out driving with them, ask them to sit in the front seat and to look out for cues on the road. You can start them on one or two cues (e.g. traffic lights and stop signs) and work up from there. By the time they go for lessons, they may have built up some confidence and competence around coordinating all the necessary activities involved in driving.

Activity 5 – Do I want to drive?

Some autistic people – and some non-autistic ones as well – will never drive. Sometimes other people will try to force them to learn, which can add to their stress. Other autistic people love driving, learn as soon as they can, and become competent and confident drivers. Other people are somewhere between those points – they may have high anxiety about learning to drive, but would really love to.

This exercise aims to assist your teen in making a choice around whether to drive or not. It is a simple but effective approach from the world of project management called a SWOT analysis. 'SWOT' stands for *Strengths, Weaknesses, Opportunities* and *Threats*.

- *Strengths* – your personal characteristics, knowledge and/or skills that are helpful.

- *Weaknesses* – things within you that are currently barriers to your achieving and succeeding and/or living well.

- *Opportunities* – external factors that can be used positively to help you achieve, succeed and live well.

- *Threats* – external factors that have the potential to be barriers to success.

Sometimes people draw this table and write lists of things in each area. This can be a very useful way to work through the thing they are considering doing – in this case, deciding whether or not to learn to drive.

	POSITIVE	**NEGATIVE**
INTERNAL	Strengths 1. 2. 3.	Weaknesses 1. 2. 3.
EXTERNAL	Opportunities 1. 2. 3.	Threats 1. 2. 3.

The analysis breaks down the decisions into a clear format. Pros and cons can also be considered after this analysis has been made. A SWOT analysis does not *make* the decision for your child, but it will help inform their decision and make the issues clearer.

LEAVING SCHOOL

Whatever someone is planning to do once they leave school, it is a huge transition point that can feel very scary for any young person. Some teenagers can't wait to leave school, whilst others would prefer to stay at school for the foreseeable future. Neither of these positions are inherently good or bad, with both having positive and negative aspects.

I really hated high school. I was bullied a lot, and I just didn't like the other students. Some of the teachers were okay, but some were useless and knew less about the things they were teaching than I did, which they seemed to be really angry with me about. I found out that I could leave school and go into a residential programme that would give me higher qualifications than I would get by staying at school. I was all set to apply when my Mum pointed out it was an army officer training college, and I was a pacifist. I hadn't thought about that aspect at all, I was just so desperate to leave. (Jo)

I loved school, and I never wanted to leave. My teachers were really nice and I had friends. I thought that if I failed my exams I could stay for another year and redo them instead of having to think about what to do next. Other people had ideas like going to college or university or getting a job and I just panicked every time I was asked what I was going to do next. Even though the careers teacher told me over and over that I could change my mind at any time, I was so worried that I would pick something that I didn't enjoy once I started doing it. (Mitch)

It is important to help your child develop an awareness of the options available to them once they leave school and to realise that they do not need to commit themselves to something forever, but can try things out. If your child is desperate to leave school, as well as looking at the options available, it can be useful to investigate why they want to leave so much. For some young people who are not academic, school can feel like a waste of time, and this information might be a useful guide to options in the future. However, for others, it may be that they feel isolated, lonely or bullied. In this case, further study may well be an option, but they may benefit from developing confidence around the social norms for different types of tertiary studies.

If your child attends a special school, they may not know what their options are post-school. A number of tertiary institutes now have transition courses available, as well as a range of study options from mostly practical to mostly theoretical, with everything in between. You might like to look at one together during the last few years that your child attends high school. In addition, there are a large number of work-experience options available in many parts of the world. These can be really useful for students on the autism spectrum in gaining an insight into exactly what work might entail, from dress codes to the actual work that gets done in that workplace.

> I loved maths at high school, and so I thought that it would be a great idea to get a job as a trainee accountant when I left school. The biggest problem with this idea was that as a trainee accountant I did very little maths and a lot of getting coffee and sandwiches for everyone else in the company. My Dad, who is an accountant, had told me that he didn't think I would like the job, but I didn't believe him. I left after just two months. The other things that really annoyed me were that I had to wear a suit, which I found really uncomfortable, and that I had to get there 28 minutes early because if I took the next train I would arrive at 9.02am, and my boss said I couldn't arrive late. (Emma)

If Emma had been able to spend a few days in an accounting firm shadowing a trainee, she would probably have decided not to do the job at all. Many young people, autistic or not, find that they can enjoy and be good at jobs that they had never thought of. However, this is not possible unless they get an opportunity to try things out. If you don't have access to a work-experience programme in your area, volunteering can be really useful.

Many young people have little or no idea what they want to do when they leave school. Some feel pressured to follow a direction that parents or others think would help them. There are many different options after school, including starting work straight away or going on to further study, which could include university, vocational education and training, apprenticeships or traineeships. Many autistic young people don't have much idea what each of these might involve and whether that option would be right for them. A lot of young people start a course or job, as Emma did in the story, and do not stay long because it doesn't live up to their expectations.

Some autistic young people do not do any work or further study after school. This can happen for a variety of reasons, such as having a traumatic experience of school and not wanting to do any more further study, a lack of confidence and direction, or poor mental health. While this is not a failing by the young person or their parents, and should result in support rather than blame, it is often a problem as it can lead to inactivity and exclusion from education and work throughout the young person's life. The teen years are very formative years, and if a teenager does not stay engaged in meaningful activities this can set up a lifetime of disengagement and poor self-confidence. In practical terms, a 30-year-old autistic person who is looking for a job and who has not completed any post-school study or employment will be at a significant disadvantage in the labour market, and may never find work or have to work at jobs that are not suited to their capability.

This is not to say that *everyone* needs to complete further study or join the workforce, but activity with an 'output' – whatever that may be – tends to be a lot more engaging and enjoyable than largely passive activities. In addition, employment provides the opportunity for greater independence, fulfilment and growth. The pinnacle of activity is not paid work, and some autistic people – and others – will be unable ever to join the workforce. However, this should be a much smaller percentage of people than it actually is. Many autistic people do not have the opportunity to undertake paid work that they would like and that they are capable of doing. Not enabling those young people to engage in further study and employment results in a waste of talent for society and a waste of potential for the autistic people who miss out. This is a complex problem, but things like further study put autistic people in a position where they are much more likely to be able to live a fulfilled and independent life.

Activities after leaving school are a significant part of a person's journey through life. Autistic young people can 'miss' those transition points for a variety of reasons. It is very important to ensure that transition points around education and career are accessible to autistic young people as well – or, if they aren't, that the young person will have the opportunity to restart their education and employment path and transitions later on.

Signs that your child is managing the transition to leaving school well include:

- They can be involved in discussions about their post-school future without high levels of stress, distress and/or anxiety.

- They are coming up with one or more options for what they would like to do when they have left school.

ACTIVITY TO HELP BUILD RESILIENCE AND CONFIDENCE AROUND LEAVING SCHOOL – OPEN QUESTIONS

This activity involves holding a session for your teen where they can ask any questions they want to around leaving school. You could also invite people your teen knows who have experience of different post-school options. This session gives your child the opportunity to ask anything they want, so will hopefully build their knowledge and help them to make an informed decision about what to do.

However, this activity has a 'hidden' element too, in that the questions your child asks will almost certainly demonstrate their concerns and worries about leaving school. This will help to inform you and will tell you what sorts of actions you need to take to support them through the process of leaving school and moving into post-school options.

TRANSITIONING TO FURTHER STUDY

Post-school study is often a great opportunity to build skills for a career and for autistic young people it can help in building confidence. Further education differs greatly from high school, and the students who are there are more likely to be genuinely interested in study and learning. Further education can be a great way to build independence and can contribute to acquiring resilience.

There are many significant differences between high school and further education. In further education, students are treated more like adults and learning tends to require more independence. Relationships with academic staff and between individual students are very different from the student–teacher dynamics in school. A university or college is a big place, both physically and socially. There is rarely the same level of support for individual students that is available in school. A higher degree of independence can be expected at university or other further-study settings and many students live at home.

While further education can be a great place for autistic students, it can also come with many challenges. Autistic students don't always complete their course, and a failed course may become a risk factor impacting on the young person's life for years to come. Supporting your young adult so that they manage well in further education and can deal resiliently with the challenges that arise is very important.

The decisions as to what course to take and in which institution to take it are very important, but other things also can impact on autistic young people's fulfilment and access in competing a course.

Signs that your young adult is doing well in preparing for further study include:

- They are actively engaged and interested in the coursework.

- If they have an interpersonal or other issue, they manage it without major disruption or extreme anxiety.

- They have some awareness of what they can manage and what they need assistance with, in terms both of coursework and of less tangible elements of study.

- A setback or an error does not result in them taking drastic action (such as quitting their course).

- Perfectionism does not result in them failing courses for not handing in work – or, if this does start to happen, they are able to address the problem by accessing assistance or through self-talk.

ACTIVITY TO COUNTER PERFECTIONISM

One issue that autistic young people can experience in school and further study – and at work too – is perfectionism. Perfectionism is essentially being very anxious about doing something and worrying that you will fail if it isn't 'perfect'. This is a big issue and can derail an autistic student's efforts from the very start. One thing that can help with perfectionism is applying perspective.

This activity can be used if your young adult child is having difficulties with perfectionism. It involves working with them to look at the worst-case scenario if their piece of work isn't 'perfect'. Then compare this to what would happen if their perfectionism means that they don't finish or submit a piece of work.

It can help if the young person makes a system for addressing perfectionism in the future. They can create a flowchart or diagram that demonstrates the outcome of either acting on the perfectionism, and the consequences of that, or handing in work even though it isn't 'perfect', and the consequences of that. While this is unlikely to address the underlying psychological issues that feed perfectionism, it is a handy practical strategy.

TRANSITIONING TO WORK

Finding employment and joining the workforce is a major life milestone for young people. Employment can give a number of positive benefits for autistic young people, including an income and through that financial independence, a sense of being part of something bigger, and learning skills and building confidence across a number of domains.

However, autistic people may struggle to find and keep employment. They can face discrimination in recruitment and at work, unhelpful assumptions about autism from employers and managers, sensory difficulties in the workplace, and difficulties feeling included socially at work. These issues can be addressed, but it pays to be aware of them.

Autistic young people preparing to join the workforce can benefit from some skills training and preparation. Important information about starting work for autistic young people relates to these aspects:

- *Choosing a job.* Knowing what kind of work they are interested in and the reason why they want a job. For example, do they just want to get some experience of employment, save some money, or start a career? These considerations will inform the kind of jobs they apply for.

- *Knowing what's expected.* They need to know the practical expectations in a paid work environment concerning matters such as taking breaks, using holiday or sick leave, and personal internet usage at work.

- *Following instructions.* They will need to follow reasonable directions and instructions from managers.

- *Applications and interviews.* They need information on recruitment and application processes, particularly CVs and interviews.

- *Unwritten rules.* They need information on the 'hidden curriculum' of employment – the unwritten rules that neurotypical employees usually know instinctively but that aren't immediately obvious to autistic people (such as rules about small talk, how the workplace hierarchy works, and topics that are suitable to discuss at work and those that aren't).

- *Dress.* The need to know about dressing 'appropriately' for work and how this varies according to each workplace and job.

- *Presentation.* They need to know about neatness, cleanliness and personal hygiene, and why these are important at work.

- *Soft skills.* The need to understand what work 'soft' skills are and why these are as essential to the job as the more technical, practical skills. Soft skills include:

  - punctuality and time management

  - enthusiasm and a work ethic

  - honesty and integrity

  - respect for colleagues from diverse backgrounds

  - a polite and courteous attitude, particularly in customer service.

A young person's first experience of employment can shape their attitude to work through life, so it is important for the first experience to be positive – or, if it isn't, to work through the issues so that knowledge from the experience can inform future work experiences and be seen as a useful experience.

Preparation is key for milestones of the kind of magnitude of starting employment. Talking about employment from several years before your child is likely to enter the workplace can be very helpful and to make employment part of their reality, even before they start to work out what job they want to do. It is also useful to see employment in terms of a journey. The first few jobs a person has are unlikely to be what they do forever, and are likely to be lower-paid and involve less complex tasks. This can help them understand that their first few jobs might not be the exact thing they want to do. Seeing employment as a journey is also helpful in terms of the young person's skill level and experience. Autistic young people often want to achieve proficiency at a task right away, and if they don't they may lose interest. In a work context this is not a very helpful attitude, but if they understand that proficiency and skills will be built over time, not right away, that understanding can help them to remain in their job and also to have a more positive attitude to their work.

It is also useful for young people to be aware that they have rights at work. This includes their pay and conditions, but also issues such as harassment, bullying and unwanted sexual attention. Teaching them their rights at work – and their responsibilities – is a good idea, including where to go if they are bullied or harassed (or if they feel that they are being bullied or harassed).

There are a number of services that can assist autistic young people to find work, from government-funded disability employment services (in some countries) to recruitment consultants and school-based employment programmes. Some of these services are better than others, and it is worth shopping around – and discussing options with other parents and young people who have used them – before choosing one.

Employment is often a challenge for autistic people. Autistic people have significantly lower employment participation and higher unemployment rates than non-autistic people, as evidenced in Australian Bureau of Statistics figures.[9] There are a number of reasons for low participation by autistics. One of these is low expectations, which can come from a variety of quarters. Some autistic young people are assumed to be unable to work even before they attempt to look for a job. Parents can be a part of countering low expectations by starting from the perspective that there is employment for almost everyone, given the right circumstances. Autistic young people may not use verbal speech, may have high anxiety, may be perfectionists and fear failure, may have co-occurring mental illness and/or intellectual disability or may have poor executive functioning, and some people may wrongly assume that they therefore cannot work – but this does not need to be the case. Employment can be tailored to an individual's skills and circumstances. Some autistic young people will be knocked back after several attempts at finding work, but this does not mean they shouldn't keep trying. While there are people who will never be able work, it is important not to start from the premise that young people won't be able to work. It is also important not to give up looking for work – and in so doing, to give up on your child's ambitions of working before even starting.

---

9   The labour force participation rate was 40.8% among the 75,200 people of working age (15–64 years) living with autism-spectrum disorders. This compared with 53.4% of working-age people with disability and 83.2% of people without disability. The unemployment rate for people with autism-spectrum disorders was 31.6%, more than three times the rate for people with disability (10.0%), and almost six times the rate for people without disability (5.3%). Australian Bureau of Statistics (2017) *Autism in Australia*. Available at www.abs.gov.au/ausstats/abs@.nsf/Latestproducts/4430.0Main%20Features752015 (accessed 5 December 2017).

Jeanette is autistic and was not diagnosed until adulthood. She moved out of home at 17 and was desperate to find work. Jeanette went to a large number of job interviews and was unsuccessful. When she did get a job, she found that she was very good at the work but didn't have a lot of confidence. Because she had struggled so much to find work and that was her first experience of working, she stayed in the job for over two years – despite the fact that she really didn't like the work or the social element of work. Jeanette thought that nobody else would employ her, despite her having acquired many useful work skills in her job and having great 'soft skills' around employment – skills that meant that when she *did* look for another job she found one quite quickly. Jeanette's lack of confidence meant that she worries about her job security even now, many years later. She would have benefited from some objective thinking around her skills and experience, but anxiety got in the way. (Jeanette)

Signs that your young adult child is managing the transition to work include:

- They express interest in jobs and in looking for work.

- They put effort and enthusiasm into looking for work.

- They are willing to challenge themselves in order to build skills and knowledge for employment.

- Employment is part of their discussions about their future.

ACTIVITIES TO HELP BUILD RESILIENCE AND CONFIDENCE AROUND TRANSITIONING TO WORK
Activity 1 – Autistic employment role models

This activity involves working with your young adult to find autistic adults who are employed, preferably in an area of work your young adult is interested in. Autistic adult role models from wider professions are also useful in this exercise. Look at the kinds of skills the role model needs in their work role; and, if possible, their earlier life and the kinds of strengths and challenges they faced. (This could either be an autistic adult personally known to your young adult or someone with a profile in society.)

Activity 2 – Role-play to practise steps in job-seeking

This activity is helpful for young people who have a lot of anxiety about the recruitment process and starting work. It involves preparing your young adult for the workforce by taking them through the steps of job-seeking about which they have concerns. It is particularly useful when thinking about job interviews and starting a job for the first time, but it can also be useful for other elements such as writing a CV, an application and a cover letter, and speaking to potential referees. You can go through all the steps as many times as your young adult needs to build confidence.

Activity 3 – Job-search journal

This can form the second step of Activity 2 or it can be a stand-alone activity. The activity involves your young adult keeping a journal – on paper or online – where they record their job search and preparation activities. They can make the journal in whatever format they choose that is most helpful. It can be a place to record jobs they are interested in, 'dream jobs', notes of their skills and any areas for improvement around the skills needed for finding work, progress in their preparation to find work, and the pros and cons of selecting different people to ask to be their referees. The journal will become a resource to refer to in the future and a repository for their knowledge around employment and job-seeking. It can be used in whatever way the young person finds most beneficial.

This activity can work particularly well for young people who are visual and creative.

Activity 4 – Employment wishlist

Have your young adult write down what jobs would they would really like to do. They can be as wacky and 'out there' as they like, providing that the activity is related to something in the real world. With your young adult, look at what kind of steps they would take on the path to those jobs on their wish list that are actual jobs. This activity is a way of linking your young adult's interests and passions with the kinds of jobs that already exist.

LIFE SKILLS FOR LEAVING HOME SUCCESSFULLY

Whether a young person is planning to live independently or in some form of supported residential living, most young people do want to leave home at some stage for a life of their own. Some families can worry about this, preferring to shelter their offspring from challenges that may prove incredibly difficult or assuming that supported accommodation options do not offer the same quality of life that remaining in their childhood home would offer.

It is important to note that many autistics go through a couple of distinct attitude shifts around leaving home. These attitudes are never wanting to leave home and wanting to leave home as soon as possible. Both attitudes are normal and natural stages of development although they can switch rapidly due to anxiety or frustration. Parents too may share the attitude of not wanting their child to leave home or wishing they had already left!

No matter what kind of living situation you think your child will eventually end up in, it is good to equip them with as many life skills as possible for successfully leaving home. At the most basic, a person needs to be able to eat, to have a roof over their head (which translates to paying rent or a mortgage, or receiving government assistance to do so), and to manage their health, including physical, sexual and mental health.

One of the activities that you as a parent can carry out is to research the different living options for your child, once they are old enough and have the desire and ability to leave home. Will your child be able to 'go flatting' (that is, to live in a house or apartment share), or will they be moving into university or college accommodation during their studies, or will they be moving into supported accommodation, or will they be receiving funding so that they can manage their own care, support workers and accommodation?

If you are planning to pay rent or buy a house for your child, it can be a good idea to work through the impacts, both negative and positive, of doing so.

- Mo was given a lot of money over the years and was told that his parents would leave him their house when they died, as they didn't expect he would ever be able to manage on his own. Mo's brother resented this, and Mo felt that this was true – that he wouldn't be able to cope. At times Mo was almost paralysed by this belief. Mo has high-level qualifications and a professional job. (Mo)

- At 14 Rick announced he was never going to leave home. One parent said that was fine; the other said there was no way he could 'live in a sleep-out at the bottom of the garden forever'. At 17 Rick went to live in a sleep-out with relatives, as he didn't like where his family had moved to. At 20 Rick moved overseas to where his family were living, but moved into student accommodation and studied to be a support worker. At 22 he went flatting with friends. Rick has minimal school qualifications and a basic qualification in support work. (Rick)

- Clara had always had a passion for New Zealand, and at age 17 moved there. She settled there permanently, got married and continues to work there. Clara is a tutor at a college. (Clara)

- Alek lived at home until he was 40, after his parents had become elderly, and then moved into a small supported accommodation unit with three other adults. He is really happy there. He goes to a day centre with many of the residents, whom he first knew when he was at school with them. He doesn't like to go out with family unless they promise to bring him back to his home afterwards! Alek requires support with all activities of daily living except eating, drinking and getting dressed. He does not use spoken language and he also has an intellectual disability. (Alek)

Signs that your young adult child is managing to build resilience about the life skills needed to leave home and the idea of leaving home include:

- They talk in a positive manner about leaving home.

- They are able both to plan what to eat and to make a meal on a regular basis.

- They can make an appointment with a doctor and attend this (with or without support), and then follow medical instructions.

- They can manage friendships and relationships, and can recover if these end.

ACTIVITIES TO HELP BUILD RESILIENCE AND CONFIDENCE AROUND LEAVING HOME

The life skills needed to successfully leave home will differ depending on the level of independence that your young adult child will have, so the activities that build them differ also. If the person will be in supported accommodation where their money and meals are managed for them, like Alek, they may not need to learn skills in this area.

First, you need to believe that your young adult child should have choices and input into their life; and second, you need to believe that they are able to make such choices. Choices do not need to be expressed verbally – non-speaking autistics can express their choices in a variety of ways. Alek expressed choices by refusing to participate or joining in with activities, and has done this since early childhood. He makes choices about what clothes he wants to wear and what he wants to eat or drink. All adults should be given the opportunity to make these kinds of choices, whether or not they can learn resilience skills around money, food and health.

MANAGING FOOD – SHOPPING, PREPARING, EATING AND CLEANING UP

In this day and age, young adults do not need to be able to cook in any traditional sense of the word – they can just remove packaging and press buttons on machines or they can eat out. The average Australian eats out two to three times per week.[10]

However, it is significantly cheaper to prepare simple meals at home, as well as being easier to control what you eat when you know what is in the food. For example, some autistics prefer to eat a high-fat, low-carb diet, whilst others prefer a low-fat or high-protein diet. This can be much easier to plan for if you are preparing your own food. Where autistics have a restricted diet, they can feel more comfortable learning to prepare this themselves over time, and may even expand their diet slightly when they are in complete control.

Microwaves and machines like thermomixers can be very helpful for young people learning to manage their own food. A basic level of literacy

---

10   Source: http//futurefood.com.au/blog/2017/1/18/eating-out-in-australia-2016-in-review (accessed 9 April 2017).

is needed to use these machines but people can also follow video recipes online, which require a low level of literacy. Being able to use a variety of cooking appliances ensures that young people have choices and greater control over their food intake. Using a toaster and a barbecue are other useful skills which can be relatively easily acquired.

When building skills in this area, however, it is often easier to start with eating, then progress to cleaning up, to preparing, and finally to shopping – otherwise it can be hard to see the link between eating a meal and shopping for something that looks completely different initially.

Eating is vital for life, and yet research has indicated that eating disorders are more prevalent in the autistic community than in other groups. Autistics can benefit from understanding the rationale behind activities, so in this case eating needs to be meaningful – autistics need to be given clear information about why they need to eat and drink. Research into interoception in autism has shown that many autistics don't have an accurate sense of thirst or hunger, so they may go under or over the recommended intake of both fluid and food. If you have not already taught your young adult the link between hydration and fluid intake, and between bowel health and food intake, now is a good time to do so. Hydration charts enable autistics with poor interoceptive awareness around thirst to hydrate optimally without needing to know that they are thirsty, as long as they understand how to use the colour and smell of urine to increase water intake or to stop drinking for a while. Bowel charts, used in conjunction with learning about how fluid and food intake can affect bowels, can help to minimise constipation, even when people have no awareness of the pain that accompanies constipation.

There are large numbers of bowel health charts (e.g. Bristol stool charts) and hydration charts available online, or you could get them from your local GP or health nurse. Choose one that is realistic and easy for your family to use and understand. Problems with interoception – lacking an awareness of things like whether they are hungry or full, need the toilet, or are warm or cold – can impact not only on autistic young people's physical health but also their mood and irritability. Research shows that many behavioural challenges improve or resolve when autistic people learn better interoceptive awareness skills.[11]

---

11   Goodall, E. (2016) *Interoception 101*. Available at http://web.seru.sa.edu.au/pdfs/Introception.pdf (accessed 5 December 2017).

ACTIVITIES AROUND MANAGING FOOD
Activity 1 – Eating with friends or family in different contexts

Many autistics struggle with food issues of one sort or another. As young people grow up, the social elements and expectations around food can change. For example, in primary or elementary school, children eat because it is snack-time or lunchtime, whereas at secondary or high school, young people start to eat together in different contexts too as a social thing. If your young adult likes food, these activities may be easier for them than if they don't, or if they only eat one kind of food.

Ask your young adult to pick two or three different places to eat lunch or a snack one Saturday or Sunday. This will be for them and yourself, and – if they wish – one or two friends. If they have never ordered food before, you may want to try this with just you a few times to practise before a friend comes too. Go to the café, restaurant or 'drive through' and look at the menu together. Work out what each of you is going to eat and/or drink. Prompt your child how to order. Non-speaking autistics can use their AAC device or pointing to order, though you may want to talk to the server or cashier beforehand to explain how your child will be communicating.

Once you have both ordered, explain how payment and service work in this particular food context, but that these may be different in different places. For example, many fast-food restaurants require you to order and pay at the counter, and then to wait around for the food to be given to you on a tray or in a bag. In other places, however, you may need to order and pay at the counter, but be served at a table; and in others you may sit at your table, order and be served there, and then pay right at the end. You may want to make up short videos or social stories or cartoon strips to act as reminders or prompts for a number of options.

On your first few times practising this activity you may want to handle the payment yourself, but after that work with your child to support them in learning how to pay, either with a pre-loaded debit/PIN card or with cash. It is much harder for people to cheat your child out of their money if they are using pay wave/chip and PIN than if they are handing over cash with no idea of how much change they should receive.

As you repeat this activity, try going to some places where your child may not like as many food items, so that they can learn, with support and guidance, to navigate the anxiety around what to eat.

I only eat potatoes, chips and bread, and I only like chips from some places. I know that some of my friends won't eat in places I like to eat, because they hate the smell of the fried food, so if we go somewhere they like, I can eat bread, and if we go where I like, they eat ice-cream! (Lola)

If your child is transferring from a school where they had packed or bag lunches to an environment where they are expected to eat in a cafeteria, this activity is very helpful in building up resilience and confidence around that situation. Cafeterias are often loud; they have lighting that can be difficult; there are competing smells; and others in the line will expect that choices be made quickly. This is why it is necessary to build up skills beforehand. In addition, resilience is needed for those times when the food your child wants is not available.

Some autistics are adventurous in their food choices, whilst others (like Lola above) are not. Many are happy to eat the same meal a number of times in a week or month or year – or indeed all the time – whilst others want more variety. It doesn't matter which is more like your child: if the food they want is not available, this will be upsetting to some degree. This is why, in this activity, you should also practise making a second and even a third choice in case the first choice is not available.

If your child is non-verbal, you may wish to make them some cards to hand to servers or cashiers. These could give their regular food or drink order, or information about how they are going to communicate. For example, if your child uses a regular menu and points to the items they want, this requires the server to look where they are pointing rather than to listen for an order.

You will know that your young adult has resilience around eating in different contexts when they are able to go to a number of different places to eat or drink and know how to manage, or what to do, if they do not like the food or drink that is on offer.

Activity 2 – Cleaning up: learning to use a dishwasher and to wash and dry dishes by hand

One of the best things about going out for food is not having to clean up. However, when your child leaves home, they still need to know how to keep their kitchen area clean and tidy. Even quite young children can learn to use a dishwasher or to wash and dry dishes by hand. No doubt many adults remember washing and drying dishes after meals from very young.

Sit down with your young adult and explain that from now on some of the household jobs that you or someone else in the house has been doing are going to be shared by them too. Explain that this is helping them to learn useful skills for when they are adults. You might use a roster, or you might use a rule such as 'If you are not the cook, then you are the dishwasher/dryer/stacker.' Be prepared for some resistance, as most young adults are not particularly motivated to do housework! However, if they do not learn when they are young, this can be a barrier to independent living or finding people to live with who are clean and tidy.

The first time your young adult washes up, or dries the dishes, or stacks or unloads the dishwasher, you may need to talk them through it or use video-modelling. Video-modelling is where you video either them or yourself doing the activity, with a voiceover of what is happening, and then they watch it to see what to do. If it is of them (you can edit out any mistakes), they can also see themselves being successful and so be confident that they can do it.

Be aware that the poor proprioception (sense of body in space) experienced by many autistics means that some dishes may get broken. This is because their depth perception can be a bit off, and they can misjudge how hard and where to place things. However, a key part of resilience in this skill area is being able to cope when something breaks, and learning how to be gentler with placement of things to minimise breakages.

Even learning how much washing-up liquid to put in the sink and how to turn the tap to the right temperature are important aspects of this life skill. For one of the authors (Emma) taps are still a stuggle but she is confident that she will eventually work out how to use them and that her struggle is not the end of the world, although it can certainly still feel like it if she is very stressed at that particular moment.

When breakages occur during this activity, demonstrate and model how to clear up the broken bits safely. (Perhaps initially don't use any china or glassware that is particularly precious to you!) Rather than just saying 'Good job', use specific praise to help your young person understand *how* they did a good job. You may find it useful to offer your young adult a choice between wearing gloves and not wearing gloves. For some autistics, touching dirty plates or having their hands in dirty dishwater can be extremely distressing. If your young adult wants to wear gloves, they may need to try a few different types before finding some that feel comfortable on their hands. Some people have a latex allergy that may not be known about, whilst others find that the soft furry texture of the inside of thicker rubber gloves is either lovely or horrendous. In addition, if the gloves get a hole in them and the wearer gets their hands wet whilst wearing the gloves, this may precipitate a meltdown unless they know that taking them off immediately and drying their hands quickly will end that sensation.

The issue of what type of cloth or scrubbing implement to use can also be of great importance to an autistic, and learning what suits their style of cleaning and their sensory preferences is part of developing resilient cleaning skills. You will know that your young adult is resilient in regard to cleaning up if they are able to manage this with good humour and no meltdowns. They should be able to indicate their preference for gloves or no gloves, to fill the sink appropriately, and to clean the dishes to a good standard.

Activity 3 – Preparing food

As a child, most of our food gets prepared for us, whether it is opening and reheating packets or a meal cooked from scratch with fresh ingredients. All families are different in the style of food that they eat, and this activity needs to match your type of family. The two authors of this book have very different styles for preparing food, neither of which is better than the other – rather each person uses a style that works for them to live with as much joy and as little stress as possible in this area.

If your young adult is likely to find joy in food preparation, then they may prefer to cook a meal using a recipe. A young person who finds chopping and stirring and experimenting stressful or distressing is likely to prefer opening packets and reheating.

Activity 3A – Reheating food

Ask your young adult to take a packet of food out of the fridge or freezer. Help them find the reheating information and to identify what the different icons on the instructions mean: microwave, oven, pan on stove/cooktop. Guide them to the instructions about removal of outer (and sometimes inner) packaging, and point out that this is different for the different reheating methods. If needed, support them in removing the packaging; otherwise ask them to do this, and then place the food in the oven/microwave/pan and set the timer/temperature/power. Show them how to remove the food from the heat safely, and – if not in the microwave – how to turn off the heat source.

Activity 3B – Making a simple meal

A boiled egg and toast or a baked potato are really easy meals to make, and are both quite cheap staples that can sustain young adults in a more nutritionally beneficial way than, say, instant noodles.

BOILED EGG

Boiling an egg requires a pot or pan, water, an egg and a timer. Either find a video for your young adult to follow or give them the following instructions:

- Get out a small pan.

- Get out an egg.

- Place the egg in the pan.

- Hold the pan under the tap and fill it with water to just above the level of the egg.

- If the egg floats to the surface, it is bad. Throw it away and put a new egg in the water.

- If the egg does not float, put the pan on the stove/cooker/ cooktop.

- Turn the heat on high for that ring (where the pan is placed).

- When the water boils (lots of bubbles coming to the surface of the water rapidly), turn the heat down so that the water is boiling gently (bubbles still coming to the surface – this is called simmering).

- Turn the heat off after 4 minutes for a soft-boiled egg and after 8 minutes for a hard-boiled egg.

- Remove the egg using a slotted spoon.

You can also turn the pan off and cover it when the water is first boiling, and leave it for 12–15 minutes depending on the size of the egg.

- Hold the egg under the tap or drop it in the sink and run cold water over the egg.

- Bang the egg on the sink to crack the shell.

- Peel the shell off.

- Place the egg on a plate.

For a hot egg, you can miss out these last four steps, put the egg in an egg cup, and chop the top off using a knife.

Toast

- Take one or two slices of bread out of the packet/bag.

- Put the bread in the toaster.

- Push the toaster handle down.

- When the toast pops up, remove it carefully.

- Place the toast on a plate.

- Butter the toast if required.

Baked potato

- Select a potato and pierce it at least four times with a fork.

- Preheat the oven to 180°C. Place potato in the oven on a baking sheet and bake for one hour, or in a microwave for 3–5 minutes, depending on the size.

- Stab it with a fork to check whether it is cooked. If not cooked, place back in for longer. An oven may crisp the skin, but a microwave will not.

- Remove the potato from the oven/microwave using oven gloves or a towel (to prevent burns to your hands) and place it on a plate.

- Cut it open and add the desired fillings – e.g. butter, cheese, vegetables, ham, or mince.

Activity 3C – Making a more complex meal

Look together at some recipes (there are excellent visual recipe books available via disability organisations, or video recipes if your child can't read) – these recipes could be online or in books. Choose one for which you already have the ingredients you need.

Make this together initially. On later occasions, hand over more and more responsibility to your child. Finally, ask your child to make one meal a week for the family. At this point they will also be able to incorporate Activity 4 into their meal preparation.

During Activity 3 it is almost inevitable that something will go wrong. This should be used as a learning moment – food mostly tastes okay even when a step got accidentally missed out, or you can often fix the mistake once you realise it has happened.

You will know that your young adult is resilient with food preparation if they are able to manage when things go wrong, and without being distressed for hours afterwards.

Activity 4 – Shopping for food and planning meals

Shopping for food can be extremely stressful for anyone, but autistics can become overwhelmed by supermarkets, especially when already stressed. There are a number of strategies to minimise the negative sensory impacts, which will vary between individuals. For example, some people simply shop online and have their groceries delivered, whilst others shop at times of the day when the supermarket is quiet. Some supermarkets have 'autism-friendly shopping hours' when the music, lights and checkout noises are all dimmed. Other people find it easier to shop at the local 'fruit and veg' shop, the local butcher, and so on. However your young adult prefers to shop, in the long term, it can be helpful to experience all types of shopping that will be available to them.

Shopping for food and planning meals essentially consists of two aspects: the actual shopping, and ensuring that what is bought is suitable for meals for the week or a few days. This can be extremely difficult for young people who are impulsive, and very simple for young people who only eat one or two food items. If your young adult is likely to struggle with this, using a shopping list (visual or written) or a menu/shopping app will be very useful. (Some of these apps even have video tutorials embedded in them to teach the user how to cook the recipe once they have bought the ingredients using the shopping list provided. Some examples of apps are CookSmart, Plan to Eat and Paprika.)

Once you have a shopping list, you can work with your young adult to help them decide which kind of shopping they prefer. Some people like walking up and down supermarket aisles, whilst others really struggle to do that and love getting their groceries delivered. Cost factors and location will also affect the options available to you.

Activity 4A – Shopping independently

Get your young adult to go to your local food store and buy two items on a list, pay for them and bring them home. You may choose to accompany them for all or part of the time.

Activity 4B – Shopping with a list

Write a shopping list, or generate one from an app, for a week of meals. Use this list to buy either online or in person from one or more shops.

Activity 4C – Shopping for a recipe

Find a recipe, generate or make a shopping list, purchase the items, and then prepare the meal for family or friends. Celebrate.

You will know that your young adult is building resilience for shopping when they are able to manage Activity 4A without a problem and Activities 4B and 4C with support and without getting overly distressed.

For these activities, using local stores can enable your child to build positive relationships with the community, where they do not feel stressed or rushed by others and where people can support them if they do become overwhelmed. You will know that your child is resilient in this context when they are okay with items on their list not being in stock and can manage without them or work out a substitute ingredient without becoming too distressed.

MANAGING HEALTH

Young adults need to learn when to seek help for their health, whether this is physical or mental.

Some autistics feel pain acutely, and may be perceived as 'drama queens' and advised to toughen up or get over it. This advice is not helpful as the brain of a person like this is perceiving the pain in the way that they are expressing it. However, they need to learn what kinds of pain require first aid as a response, which require a trip to the GP or family doctor, and which require emergency treatment. One way to do this is by teaching them to ask themselves whether it is a *minor ow*, a *big ow* or a serious *major ow*.

Other autistics have what is described as high pain tolerance, but is actually poor interoceptive awareness of pain. These autistics may break a bone and not notice, which can lead to health complications. If this describes your young adult, it is important that you teach them to check themselves after an accident or incident, and to know what physical signs or symptoms require a medical response (e.g. bruising and swelling versus minor bruising, bleeding in spurts, or bleeding in a trickle).

Following on from this, it is important that young adults know how to access health care, including how to make a medical appointment. This can often be done online now, so if they dislike or do not speak on the phone, they can still make an appointment for themselves. Once an appointment has been made, they need to be able to get to the clinic or to ask for assistance in getting there. Finally, they need to be able to indicate to health professionals what the problem is, and then to understand and follow any instructions they receive from health professionals. You or a support worker may need to work with your child and their health-care practitioners to ensure that communication is two-way, especially if your child struggles to communicate pain or illness.

ACTIVITIES AROUND MANAGING HEALTH
Activity 1 – Visiting the GP/family physician

When you next need to take your young adult to the GP or family doctor, support them in making the appointment themselves, whether this is online, on the phone, or in person (using their AAC device, if appropriate). At the appointment, encourage them to be the primary communicator, using whatever communication method they find most comfortable. Make sure to book a longer appointment than would normally be needed, so that they have time to feel safe and communicate.

Check that the doctor has understood your child and that they understand the doctor. Encourage them to advocate for themselves – for example, if they do not like to be touched, they can ask that they are warned first if the doctor needs to touch them.

Activity 2 – Learning what to do in an emergency

Enrolling in a first-aid course can be really useful for young adult autistics so that they know what to do in an emergency. These courses are often taught using a combination of role-modelling and practical application tasks that suit a lot of autistic learning styles. If there are no first-aid classes in your location, you could watch some online videos and practise bandaging and so on.

If possible, ensure that your young adult knows how to call the emergency services and how to convey relevant information.

Activity 3 – The accident and emergency room/department

On a day and at a time when the emergency department closest to you is not too busy, arrange to visit. If possible, meet with one of the nurses or ward staff who can help your child to become familiar with the hospital emergency department or 'accident and emergency'. This is important because it would be much harder if their first experience of the emergency department were during an actual emergency.

You will know your child is developing resilience around managing their health when they are able to make a medical appointment even when the receptionist or online booking system cannot give them an appointment on the day or at the time they want. In addition, resilience can include their being able to accept help from and work collaboratively with health professionals in managing any long-term physical or mental health issues that your child may experience.

MANAGING SEXUALITY AND SEXUAL HEALTH

Many parents avoid discussions around sexual health as they are unsure of when and how to address this subject. If you, as the parent, are not on the autism spectrum yourself, it can also be hard to understand what your child needs to have explained explicitly and what they already know. Emma Goodall's book, *The Autism Spectrum Guide to Sexuality and Relationships: Understand Yourself and Make Choices that are Right for You*, may help you to understand the difficulties that young adult autistics can encounter when coming to terms with their sexuality and sexual health.

Sexual health is not just about engaging in safe sex rather than risky sex: it is also about having sexual health check-ups at a clinic or doctor's surgery. Your young adult will need to understand that sexual health clinics exist and what they can use them for. They may be asexual or otherwise not interested in having sexual relationships, and that is okay. Or they may be interested in sexual relationships, and that too is okay, once they are over the legal age of consent. Some disability or sex-education organisations have specific staff who work with young people on the autism spectrum or with other disabilities, so you may want to see what is available in your area.

The teen years are often a time of emerging discovery of sexuality and learning who you are – your identity – in terms of gender. While emerging sexuality in their children can make many parents want to pretend it isn't happening, in fact teens – autistic or not – are discovering and exploring their sexuality. In essence this is usually perfectly okay and natural and good, but it can come with some challenges for autistic young people. Sex has both physical and emotional elements. These elements may be disconnected for autistic young people, resulting in a variety of difficulties. There are often expectations from peers that young people should be sexually active, and autistic teens who have not had their first sexual encounter may feel pressured into doing so just to be able to say that they have.

There are some important considerations around sexual activity, and you will need to talk with your child to make sure they are aware of what is and what isn't consensual, and that they have the right to say no to anything they don't want to do sexually.

Autistic young people have the same range of sexualities and gender identities as other young people. A significant number of autistic people are transgender or gender-divergent. Sexuality and gender are very deeply experienced, personal things. For autistic teens who are likely to be coming to terms already with a number of elements around identity, considerations around gender and sexuality may add some more 'big things' to think about. This can be an overwhelming time for your teen, especially if they are discovering that their sexuality and/or gender identity is not the 'expected' one of heterosexuality and cis gender.

Divergent sexuality and gender identity can be used by bullies as a means to attack and ridicule an autistic teen. This can increase the risk of violence to the autistic teen and suicidal ideation. Nobody should be shamed for their gender identity or sexuality, but all too often they are. Gender-diverse autistic young people are particularly vulnerable to being attacked and bullied. It should be noted that this is not the fault of the autistic young person. Bullying is a choice made by the bully: while bullying is a complex issue, it is still the bully's choice to attack their victim and not the victim's 'fault' for appearing different.

Shaming and prejudice around gender identity and sexuality can sometimes come from family members. This may be experienced by the autistic teen as being far worse than attacks by school bullies. The young person may feel unable to authentically express who they are at school or at home or anywhere else. Even if parents struggle with their child being trans or having a non-heterosexual sexuality, they need to move past that and support their child. The place of safety should not come to an end because the child does not conform with the expected gender or sexuality. Your child deserves love and support regardless of their sexuality and gender.

For autistic young people who are transgender, there are a number of additional things they – and their parents – need to consider and navigate. For parents, considerations include things such as where to go for advice and support for their child and themselves, where to find peer support for their child, how to find a clinic or doctor in their area who is expert in gender dysphoria and autism, information, and potentially also legal requirements (e.g. changing birth certificates and other identification). There is a lot of prejudice and misinformation about transgender experience and parenting trans kids. This can impact on both parents and their trans child. Young people may take on board unhelpful attitudes about themselves which can impact their self-esteem and identity. Always keep in mind, and express to your kids, that any child – including an autistic child, a trans child or a gay child – is worthy of love and respect, and your child is a valuable and valued member of your family and the community, whatever bigots might say.

When Molly was 16, she went away with some older friends. Molly was quite rebellious and often argued with her parents. She was very keen to leave home and be an adult, but, like many autistic young people, she was quite naive and assumed that other people were all as kind and thoughtful as she was. She couldn't imagine anyone being deliberately rude or saying nice things but meaning unpleasant things.

When she was away with the older friends whom she didn't know all that well, one of the men, who was in his late thirties, gave her a beer. She felt very grown up. He gave her another, and she felt a bit light-headed. Then he talked to her about sex and how beautiful and natural it was. She wasn't sure if she wanted to go with him to have sex or not when he asked her, but she thought it was very adult and mature to have sex, so she

did, even though she didn't enjoy it and felt very guilty about it. Afterwards she wished she had said no to the man and felt regret that her first sexual experience had been so confusing. She never knew if it was consensual – it sort of was and sort of wasn't. She didn't tell anyone for several years as she felt ashamed. (Molly*)
[*Used with permission from 'Molly']

Signs that your child is doing well with issues around their gender and sexuality include:

- They are willing to speak to you about their sexuality or gender identity, and are comfortable in doing so.

- They are happy to talk to you about – or to introduce – a boyfriend or girlfriend.

- They do not demonstrate self-hatred or negativity around themselves in terms of their sexuality, gender identity or sexual interests.

- They do not engage in relationships or sexual encounters to prove themselves to peers (such as proving to peers that they are neither a virgin nor asexual, or proving that they are heterosexual).

- They are respectful of others' sexuality and gender identity.

- They do not engage in sexually aggressive or violent behaviour themselves.

ACTIVITIES AROUND SEXUAL HEALTH, SEXUALITY AND GENDER
Activity 1 – 'The talk'

This activity is valuable as it shows that you, as a parent, can ensure that your adolescent is comfortable sharing things with you and asking for help.

The talk is about getting to know how your adolescent is doing in coming to terms with their changing body, whether that is growing hair, developing breasts, or having unexpected erections or wet dreams. Once you know how comfortable they feel in their body, you can gauge whether or not to introduce information about masturbation and/or sexual activities. For some young adult autistics, a lack of knowledge about sex and masturbation can lead to pregnancy and/or disease if they did not know that 'that' was sex.

Activity 2 – Role-modelling healthy relationships

Hopefully, you will have been role-modelling healthy relationships for most of your child's life, but for various reasons this is not possible all the time for many people. However, it is important to note that autistics are abused at higher rates than other people, and a lack of understanding about what constitutes a healthy or an unhealthy relationship contributes to this.

Activity 3 – Discussing and appraising friendships and possible relationships

It is helpful to honestly appraise your own and your young adult's friendships and possible relationships. This can help them to understand when people are worth being around and when they are better off without particular people. Depending on the emotional and social maturity of your young adult, you may need to use social stories, cartoons or emoticons to evaluate people's attributes. Be very specific – for example: 'John was not nice to you when he took all your money to buy everyone ice creams. This was not nice, because he was taking advantage of you and did not ask you if it was okay.'

Activity 4 – Discussing different types of relationships and how to manage break-ups

It can be very hard for autistics to navigate the minefield of teenage relationships, where young people are 'going out' with each other one day and 'broken up' the next, never having been anywhere! If you do not discuss relationships with your adolescent they will be reliant on information from school and online, which may or may not be accurate. Again, if you are not comfortable doing this, there are a myriad of books or videos on the subject, even if you want very specific information for young adults with autism and/or intellectual disability.

A very important part of resilience when growing up is being able to manage when a relationship ends. Even if the relationship was not particularly long and did not involve many interactions, autistics can become intensely attached in a very short space of time and, like most young people, they may feel devastated that things do not go well.

When their first 'relationship' ends, a natural thought for many autistics is that 'I will never have another relationship again – no-one will ever love me again.' This catastrophising is not helpful, but it is more a case of the 'now' seeming like 'forever' than of making a small problem into a huge one. It can be helpful to work through other changes that have happened and how nothing ever stays the same forever – for example, in pre-school they made friends with someone, then they stopped being friends, and then they made another friend. Accept their feelings around the break-up whilst helping them manage their attitude to the permanency around their state of being.

Activity 5 – Providing information about sexual health and sexual health check-ups

If your young adult is sexually active or if you think they soon may be, it is important that they have access to sexual health information in an accessible format. You may choose to take them to a sexual health clinic or to meet with your family doctor or you could provide them with written or video information.

You will know that your child is building resilience around their sexual health when they can indicate that they need medical support or management and can engage with that collaboratively. In addition, they will be doing well if they can make decisions about whether to be involved in a relationship or not, and how to behave in that relationship; and if when a relationship ends they are not devastated for a long period of time.

Activity 6 – Consent

Consent is possibly the most important consideration around sex and sexuality. You do not want your child to be the victim of abuse or rape; and you also don't want your child to be a perpetrator of sexual violence just because they didn't know about consent.

This activity involves asking your child a series of questions about things you want them to do. Make some of the questions about things you know they would really enjoy, and other questions about things you know they would *not* want to do. Ask why they would or wouldn't want to do each thing. You can then talk about sex and relate it to the things your child really wanted and those they didn't. Ask them how they would feel if you made them do one of the things they really didn't want to, regardless of what they said. Using this example, explain that with sexual activity there are similar issues. If someone tells you they do not want you to do something, you always have to take notice of that, because it is their body to make decisions about. You can also include some 'rules' around sex – things that it is never okay to do, such as having sex with someone who is unconscious or drunk; or ignoring their sexual partner when the partner says no to what they want to do (even if they think it is okay); and that even though someone is their partner/boyfriend/girlfriend, they still have the right to say no to sexual activity.

Activity 7 – Gender (for teens who are trans, non-binary gender, or questioning their gender identity)

If your child has expressed that they are transgender or non-binary gender, they need to know that you love, value and support them. Aim to be their strongest supporter and ally. Even if you think this ought to be obvious from your responses to them, they may still be anxious because how you feel may not be clear to them. Autistic people often struggle to recognise facial expressions and body language and may only take meaning from the words you say or write, so even though you may feel that your love and support are clearly evident, your child may not. This may also be compounded by their own view of themselves, which may be critical. They may be being bullied at school around gender or sexuality, and that can impact on how they respond to your statements about sexuality and gender. If you have said negative things about gender identity in the past, your child may have held onto that for a long time. A throwaway comment several years ago may mean that your child is now terrified of talking to you about their gender identity.

This activity simply involves saying to your child clearly and in unambiguous language that you value and support them, and that you are always there for them. Explain that if there are elements of their life where there may be prejudice or bigotry (such as at school or if any relatives are narrow-minded and upsetting for your child), you are there for them. Work together with them to build their positive self-perception as a gender-divergent or trans person. If they are questioning their gender, do not dismiss their view that they might be trans, or even their idea that they might not be. You can introduce them to role models who are autistic and trans or gender-divergent. These include advocates Dr Wenn Lawson and Roe Renee. If you yourself know autistic and/or gender-divergent adults or young people, you could arrange a meeting if your child would like that. The important things here are 'normalising' the experience of gender diversity and questioning gender, and being available as a supporter and an ally.

CHAPTER 6

FAILING SUCCESSFULLY

WHY FAILING WELL IS A VITAL SKILL

Being able to fail well is an essential life skill for every single person. Being able to acknowledge a mistake and then move on is a very useful strategy and makes it easier to take on challenges, try new things and learn important lessons. However, many autistic young people are perfectionists and really struggle with this concept. Instead of simply acknowledging a problem and moving on, they may initially be traumatised by making a mistake or failing to manage something. Being able to fail successfully is skill that translates across all elements of life. Successful failing is a core element of building resilience and 'bouncing back' from setbacks. Failing successfully is a skill which autistic preteens, teens and young adults can learn and which will help them in building their resilience and independence.

Most people do not enjoy failure. It is frustrating, disappointing and stressful. For autistics, particularly for children and young people, their predisposition to perfectionism means that failure can be traumatic and can lead to feelings of inadequacy and self-criticism. Combined with the negative messaging they may have received around their capability, failing can result in autistic teens and young adults giving up even before they start. Failure and mistakes can also become caught up with anxiety and fear of change. Autistic young people can become so worried about getting something wrong that this heightens their anxiety around the task, which may contribute to a failure, which will further compound their anxiety and may result in them refusing to try again. Fear of failure can work against resilience and independence as teens may be unwilling to take on new tasks for fear of failing or of looking stupid in the eyes of anyone else. Perfectionism and performance anxiety are significant risk factors around failing successfully.

In a sense, resilience can be viewed as the opposite to fear of failure and is a useful resource for a perfectionist. To take on a new task or challenge in an effort to build resilience requires some understanding that in most cases failure is not 'the end of the world'. If a young person is too anxious about failing to take on an activity or task, then it will be harder for them to build their resilience and independence. As children and teens get older and approach adulthood, the window of opportunity for learning to fail well gets smaller. For this reason, understanding issues around mistakes and failure is at the heart of supporting autistic young people in becoming more resilient.

Parents play a significant part in lessening the fear of failure and in supporting their autistic kids in taking on new challenges. Throughout your child's journey to adulthood it is important to model failing so that they can gain an understanding that *everyone* makes mistakes or fails from time to time, and it is rarely catastrophic.

> When I was 17, I was in my final year of high school. All my classmates were 18 and legally allowed to drink alcohol, which I wasn't. At the end of the year my classmates all went to a bar to celebrate. I wanted to come too but knew I wouldn't be allowed in the club without ID showing I was 18. One of my classmates who didn't look like me at all lent me her driving licence to use as ID. When I got to the club, the bouncer saw the licence and that it definitely wasn't me. She told me quite loudly to 'get out!' That would have been fine, but a police car had just pulled up. The police gave me a $50 fine for using fake ID. I was so mortified by this I couldn't tell anyone about it for years. I don't think anyone else involved – the friend with the ID, the bouncer or the police officers – would have remembered the incident after only a couple of years, but I still feel embarrassed thinking about it. (Jenny)

In the story above, if Jenny had been more comfortable about making mistakes, and had understood that mistakes can be good sources of new knowledge and learning, she might have responded quite differently.

FAILURE AND MISTAKES ARE INEVITABLE

There is a saying that 'to err is human'. Every single one of us will make mistakes and fail, often many times over. Autistic people can be highly anxious about making a mistake, but inevitably one is going to occur at some point. It is important to convey this message and that failure and setbacks are part of life and that they are usually okay.

There is a scale of magnitude for errors and failure. Recognising how significant the error is may determine their response. For example, forgetting their school bag is an error with a small impact – the young person will not have their books and other things they need for one day at school. This error would best be viewed as a learning opportunity: you could encourage your child to develop a system for ensuring that they pack everything they need for school and remember to take their bag.

A more challenging mistake might be where the young person has misread cues from somebody to whom they are attracted and sent that person a large number of messages, even after the recipient and their parent/s have asked them not to and have explained that these made the recipient feel uncomfortable or threatened. This is a mistake that has consequences for the object of the autistic young person's affection, and that could have very serious repercussions for both young people. The recipient of the texts would probably be scared and feel very uncomfortable. Even if the intent was not stalking, the person receiving the messages would not have known that, and the impact on them might be very similar to their reaction had this indeed been genuine stalking. Even finding out 'after the fact' that the messaging was the result of a misunderstanding may not stop the recipient of the messages from feeling invaded and harassed. Unless the young person has some support in addressing the error and learning from their mistake, this may become a damaging memory and a source of self-hatred for years to come. If they do not understand the impact on the person who received the messages, it may also make them less aware of such consequences and they may struggle with knowing the impact of their actions on others, which in the extreme form may result in criminal behaviour in adulthood. It is important to work through this kind of error and to help the young person understand that everyone makes errors. In this instance, the error could either be seen as entirely negative or it could be used to help the young person avoid similar issues in the future.

Convey the idea that everyone makes mistakes and that remorse, regret, embarrassment or shame are the usual feelings people experience in these kinds of situations, and it is perfectly okay for your child to feel this way. It is helpful if you can also convey the importance of accepting that the incident happened – it is not helpful for the young person to keep 'beating themselves up' about it. Another learning from this sort of experience is to acknowledge the impact of actions on the other person affected. In the example here, an apology to the person the messages were sent to might be a good step, or, if that isn't possible, it may help to spend some time reflecting on how the error impacted the other person and how remorse may be used to help avoid a similar situation in the future. Apologies, however, do need to be genuine. You cannot force your child to apologise, and in fact if you did it would most likely backfire, as nobody wants to receive a fake, forced apology. Indeed, a forced apology often makes matters worse rather than better. You can encourage your child to apologise and support them in doing so, after they have reflected on the consequences of their actions and how they would feel in a similar situation.

MAKING FAILURE USEFUL

Instead of dwelling on the mistake or failure and the young person's 'poor behaviour', it is much better for parents to move from guilt and discipline into the constructive space of successful failure, whereby the young person learns from what went wrong. Parents can work through what went wrong, why it happened, and how their child could manage similar situations in the future. The discussion needs to be constructive and focused on building understanding of what went wrong and why, and how to avoid it happening again. Parents need to avoid blaming and shaming and focus on scaffolding solutions, so that the young person develops an understanding that they made an error which had consequences, and that they can learn from this for the future. With teens and young adults these reflective skills can be taught, so that next time there is a mistake the young person themselves might be able to work though how to turn the experience into a constructive one. Parents can assist their child in this.

For young people who have difficulties with cognition or with understanding consequences, this message may need to be simplified: 'Next time this happens, do this.' Video-modelling the situation being handled successfully by a sibling, a peer or a parent can support this learning for young adult autistics.

Ideally the discussion should avoid producing a burden of nebulous anxiety and guilt, just as it should avoid provoking defiance. The young person will hopefully learn a constructive lesson from their mistake, and this will enable them not to make the same mistake again and to understand how to avoid similar mistakes in related areas. Successful failure should ideally be an ongoing process, similar to developing resilience, which builds on previous experience and understanding.

In high school I had one friend. He was the school's drug dealer. I thought that it was okay to deal drugs, but then I watched *Breaking Bad*, and I saw all the things that can go wrong. So, when my friend asked me to sell drugs too, I said no, it was wrong. He was really angry with me and said if I was his friend I would. I remembered what my teacher said in Year 4 when someone in my class got me to throw a chair by saying that I would do it for him if I really liked him. My teacher said that when people say that they don't mean it, and if they tell you they won't like you anymore because you won't do something, they didn't like you in the first place. So, I said that I couldn't be friends anymore. I felt sad, like I would never make a friend again, but at the same time I was proud I learnt from my mistakes in Year 4. (John)

WHAT DOES SUCCESSFUL FAILURE LOOK LIKE IN AUTISTIC PRETEENS, TEENS AND YOUNG ADULTS?

Learning to fail successfully is usually an incremental process. As with resilience more broadly, it is good to start thinking about strengthening your child's ability to handle setbacks and failure as early as you can.

Aged 11–15 years

At the ages of 11–15 years, failing successfully might include being able to:

- keep going with an activity they didn't succeed at initially

- set and maintain goals despite setbacks

- be able to understand on some level what went wrong and why

- be able to discuss the mistake or setback and work through any shame or embarrassment

- apologise, with some prompting if required, after poor behaviour or interpersonal issues where they made the wrong choice

- demonstrate over the coming days/weeks/months that on some level they have learned from the experience.

Aged 16–20 years

At the ages of 16–20 years, failing successfully might include being able to:

- work through or discuss the failure or setback with a parent or trusted adult

- take on board constructive criticism

- understand why the mistake happened and how to avoid repeating it in the future

- demonstrate learning from the mistake and transferring that understanding to other areas

- make a genuine apology to someone who was negatively impacted by a mistake

- understand the impact of mistakes on others

- understand the different magnitudes of errors and use that knowledge to address and learn from the mistake.

CHALLENGES FOR AUTISTIC YOUNG PEOPLE AROUND FAILING

Failure and mistakes happen for all people at all ages. Typically, all developing young people can also struggle with mistakes – it is not an experience unique to autistics. However, autistic young people may have some additional challenges around failing, including these:

- Failing may compound anxiety around an activity.

- Failing may feed insecurity and self-doubt, leading to a negative self-perception and a lack of confidence in attempting the activity at which they failed again or attempting new activities. That may be a significant risk factor for lacking resilience and independence.

- Failing is incredibly hard for someone who is a perfectionist. Perfectionism can cause a kind of action paralysis which means that the young person will not do anything or finish tasks unless they consider the outcome to be perfect. For a perfectionist, failure may be their biggest fear. This means that failure can feed into perfectionism and vice versa.

- Autistic young people may try to avoid failure or mistakes at any cost, which can cause significant anxiety and halt any work on building their resilience.

- Autistic young people may not take on a new activity for fear of failing at it.

- Autistic young people may relive errors and setbacks and go over the error with the accompanying feelings of shame and remorse. This affects their self-esteem and confidence, and can lead to self-criticism and a negative view of themselves and their capability.

IMPACTS OF NOT BEING ABLE TO MANAGE FAILURE WELL

Not being able to successfully manage failure or making mistakes may be associated with a range of challenges and difficulties, including increasing the risk of anxiety, depression and mental illness.

In autistic children and teens, not being able to manage failure and mistakes can mean:

- They may feel unable to take on any new tasks or activities or to revisit things that have been unsuccessful in the past.

- They may feel the need to be proficient at a task immediately. If this does not occur, they may abandon the task. This can look as though they are being oppositional. However, responding to this task refusal as oppositional behaviour does not work well in addressing this belief and can actually compound the issue.

- Perfectionism and anxiety may increase.

- They may avoid social situations due to previous faux pas and/or embarrassment.

- They may show only limited or no understanding of the consequences of their own behaviour.

- They may feel attacked or harassed by adults who are focused on an error that the young person doesn't think is a 'big deal'.

- They may be unable to respect and/or set limits and boundaries.

- They may refuse to go to school, not wanting to see people who have witnessed errors or poor behaviour, and may experience difficulties in maintaining friendships.

- They may not attend a higher education course or start employment due to embarrassment or shame around an error.

- They may feel self-doubt and insecurity.

- They may find it difficult to acquire independent living skills.

- They may be afraid of engaging socially.

- They may withdraw, and may develop a gaming/internet addiction.

- They may have low educational attainment.

- They may be unemployed, being unable to join the workforce.

It should be noted that factors other than difficulty in failing, including external factors, can also result in or contribute to these issues.

TEACHING AUTISTIC CHILDREN AND YOUNG PEOPLE TO FAIL SUCCESSFULLY

Failure and mistakes are best viewed as an opportunity to learn lessons and move on. A parent's attitude and response to failure can strongly influence how a young person feels about making mistakes and failing. Where the negative aspect of a failure or mistake is emphasised by parents, and the prevailing attitudes are those of blame, recrimination and criticism, a child or teen is more likely to cope poorly with failure. Even if the parent is supportive and/or does not apportion blame, autistic children and teens can still struggle if the parent places a lot of emphasis on the failure itself rather than on how the mistake can become a useful learning experience.

When I was learning to get the bus by myself, I got completely lost in the bus station after school and missed the bus home. There weren't any other buses, and I had to call my mum and ask her to come and collect me when she finished work. She said it was really good that I called and a good solution to my predicament. When she picked me up, she wanted to talk about what I would do if she couldn't pick me up and if there was a way to make sure I didn't miss the bus. I missed it another couple of times in the next year, but I got much more confident about using the buses and even went to cadets by myself on the bus when we moved to a new house. (Jack)

Attitudes to failure can be viewed either with a past-focused or a future-focused approach. When you are *past-focused*, you are looking back to the mistake; why the young person did the wrong thing, what the consequences were, and so on. For most people, including non-autistic people, this approach often makes it hard to move on from an error. When you approach the mistake from a *future-focused* position, it can be used as the basis of learning lessons and strategies for the future. Acknowledge what happened and allow your child to apologise, or to make reparations if that is required. Then shift the focus to looking forward from the mistake into the future. The mistake is not something to dwell on, but something to learn from. This can help enable your child to fail successfully and to start to learn to 'make adversity their teacher', as in the example above from Jack.

TALKING WITH YOUR CHILDREN AND YOUNG PEOPLE ABOUT SUCCESSFUL FAILURE

If your child fails at something or makes a mistake, talk about why it happened and how they can address the issue in the future. Keep blame out of the conversation as much as possible – both your own blame and your child's self-admonishment. You can tailor your message depending on your child's age, personality, learning style and approach, and level of cognitive capacity.

Don't forget that many mistakes happen because the child or teen is doing things for the first time or doing things of which they have little knowledge or experience. Blaming them for failure in these sorts of circumstance is unhelpful and can result in them being less willing to try new things in the future. In fact, errors and setbacks resulting from doing new things offer an excellent opportunity for them to learn from these errors and make use of that learning when doing similar things in the future. This learning, and acquiring helpful strategies through understanding the reason for an error, is the essence of failing successfully.

Here are some practical ways to help your child or teen learn to fail successfully:

- *Validate them.* It is easy for parents and other adults to criticise a child or teen when they have apparently behaved poorly or acted without thinking. It is easy to focus on the behaviour or the error. This is not necessarily a problem in itself, but the child or young person also needs validation from parents in order to turn the messaging around their mistake into something that helps them move forward and avoid that mistake in the future. If your messaging is all blame and discipline and no validation, it may result in them having a negative view of themselves and may impact on their self-esteem and self-worth. These attitudes are in fact counterproductive in terms of your child's resilience journey. Autistic children and young people particularly can be very prone to this kind of all-or-nothing response to discipline. It is important for them to know that you are displeased with the *error* they made, but not with *them* per se. In Jack's story, his mum validated his problem-solving and then looked at how to prevent the issue in the future.

- *Don't shame your child.* Autistic kids and young people are often in tune with the emotions of others and may have a lot of self-doubt, identity issues and/or self-hatred. If a parent or trusted adult belittles or shames an autistic child or young person, this is not constructive or helpful and may well result in heightened issues with perfectionism and fear of taking on new challenges. In the example above, Jack's mum did not embarrass him or shame him for missing his bus: instead she saw and exploited the learning opportunity.

- *Help them to evaluate consequences.* Autistic people can become very caught up in guilt and regret and how they are doing things 'wrong'. Even if their parent is supportive and positive, they may still beat themselves up emotionally over and over again following a failure. In this instance, parents can help their child unpack the error and how the consequences are not as bad as they think. Working on other psychological issues can also be of assistance. Anxiety and perfectionism frequently lead the person to dwell on errors, so interventions to assist with these issues can help. The thinking style that many autistics have, of perseverating on mistakes, can be challenged through the use of reflections on solutions achieved in the day.

- *Recognise misunderstandings.* It is important to note that actions or behaviour seen as 'mistakes' by schools and by society more broadly can often be the result of misunderstandings between autistic and non-autistic styles of communication. An autistic child or teen might do something 'wrong' in response to a genuine concern or a misunderstanding. Some autistic children and teens can go through school being seen as rebellious or difficult when in fact that was not their intent. Sometimes this misinterpretation of behaviours can lead to an autistic child or teen assuming a rebellious persona simply because that is how they are viewed by others.

- *Develop coping strategies.* You can help your child build their toolbox of coping strategies when an error or a setback does occur, and work through processing responses (theirs and yours) to the error or setback and its implications.

EXERCISE AROUND UNDERSTANDING RESPONSES TO ERRORS

Ethan, a 14-year-old autistic boy, has a crush on a girl in his English class, Tanika. Ethan is not very competent at English and was really struggling with the book they were reading for their class. One lunchtime the two of them had a long conversation about the book. Tanika knew a lot about the book and asked Ethan if he would like to come over to her house, so that she could help him with the assignment. Ethan thought this meant Tanika was interested in him romantically as well, but in fact Tanika only wanted to assist Ethan with his homework because he always seemed to be struggling with English assignments. She thought she had explained that to Ethan by mentioning her boyfriend a couple of times. When Ethan went to her house, he wore his nicest clothes and brought flowers, thinking that the homework session was in fact a date. Tanika was surprised but responded quite respectfully, explaining that Ethan had made an error of judgement but reassuring him it was okay and that she understood. Despite her response, Ethan was very embarrassed and angry with himself for making this error. He couldn't even think about the error for several weeks without the memory causing him severe shame and embarrassment.

Ethan first stopped going to his English class and has now stopped going to school at all, feeling horrified that he got a social situation with someone he looked up to and wanted to like him so 'wrong'.

Questions

- What sorts of things would have contributed to Ethan's quite extreme reaction to his 'error'?

- What would be some things Ethan's parent/s and teachers could do to help him manage his anxiety and embarrassment to the extent that he would be comfortable returning to school?

- How could this situation be framed as a learning experience for Ethan?

BUILDING SELF-ESTEEM AND SELF-CONFIDENCE FOR AUTISTIC CHILDREN AND YOUNG PEOPLE

When I was 16, a neighbour asked me to go over to his house to see his hamster, which he said he kept in his room. When I got to his room, there was no hamster, and he started to take his clothes off, saying he was really happy I wanted to have sex with him. I didn't want this at all and had no idea why he would think this, so I ran home and hid in my room. I tried to avoid him forever after that. Years later I still don't understand what I did wrong, but now I know that it wasn't my fault and I don't need to be ashamed or embarrassed about it. (Lily)

Children and young people who have good self-esteem are often more confident in how they approach life and may be less likely to be really distressed by a mistake or setback. As you support and encourage your child's resilience, they are likely to become more able to recover from making a mistake or failing. Self-confidence, self-esteem, resilience and successful falling can all be seen as part of a positive dynamic. The elements can feed into each other and strengthen your child's ability to manage setbacks, challenges, change and adversity. A great starting point is to build your child's level of self-esteem.

The kidshealth.org website defines 'self-esteem' as having a good opinion of yourself and feeling good about yourself as a person.

People with self-esteem:

- feel valued and accepted by others

- feel worthy of being treated with fairness and respect

- accept and respect themselves, even when they make mistakes

- believe in themselves, even when they didn't succeed at first

- see their own good qualities, such as being kind, capable, or fun to be around

- take pride in the things they do, like passing a difficult maths test or mastering a new recipe

- think positively about themselves.[12]

WHAT DOES SELF-ESTEEM LOOK LIKE?

For autistic children and young people, self-esteem may look a little different from self-esteem in their typically developing peers. Given the challenges many autistic children and young people face, what their parents need to know about supporting and promoting their self-esteem may be different from the knowledge needed by parents of typically developing children. For many autistic children self-esteem is very fragile. Bullying and exclusion, combined with extreme anxiety around social faux pas and revisiting negative experiences, can mean that an autistic young person's self-esteem takes hit after hit. It is vital to address this, as low self-esteem often results in significant difficulties in building a positive identity, independence and resilience.

The activities in this book form part of building your child's level of self-esteem, along with resilience. Other actions parents can take to boost self-esteem include:

12 Source: http://kidshealth.org/en/teens/about-self-esteem.html (accessed 5 December 2017).

- Making sure that your young person feels included in the family. This is of particular relevance for teens who are going through a time of rebellion and/or who have difficulties interacting with other family members.

- Validating and supporting them – being 'in their corner', especially in difficult times.

- Emphasising their strengths and skills, and not focusing on errors and deficits.

- Loving them in a way that makes sense to them.

- Celebrating their achievements and making sure that the celebration is genuine and sincere and meaningful to your child.

- Maintaining their sense of a place of safety throughout their preteen, teenage and young adult years.

- Understanding them and not punishing them for things that might be perceived as poor behaviour but are in fact reactions to bullying or injustice or the result of overload/meltdown or mental health difficulties.

- Setting boundaries and limits that support them in building their skills around interacting with others and negotiating the social world. This is very important.

- Taking an interest in their interests.

- Encouraging them and supporting them in engaging with positive things, such as study and work.

- Being honest with them and aiming to be someone they can trust and confide in.

- Demonstrating that you value them as they are, and providing support for their identity as an autistic person.

- If they are gender-divergent or transgender or express that they are non-heterosexual, support them. Bullying around sexuality and gender is rife in society, so it is vital that your child feels they can confide in you and be supported by you as they develop their understanding around their gender identity and/or sexuality.

- Enabling them to find a peer group, whether that is interest-based or neurodiversity-based.

CHALLENGES TO SELF-ESTEEM FOR AUTISTIC CHILDREN AND YOUNG PEOPLE

Challenges to self-esteem are often similar to the challenges or risk factors around resilience. Invalidation and having their concerns dismissed often pose significant challenges to self-esteem for autistic children and young people. Adult role models who focus only on deficits and problems can also be a threat to their self-esteem, and this can follow a young person throughout their life. They may spend their lifetime trying to gain the approval of a parent whose behaviour and outlook suggest that they would prefer their child not to be – or not to seem – autistic.

Having their natural way of being and experiencing the world invalidated can also damage the self-esteem of autistic children and young people. For example, when an autistic teen says that it is noisy in their classroom and their teacher says it is not, that is because the teacher's hearing is less sensitive than the teen's – but this response invalidates their experience.

Learning to advocate for themselves is one of the best ways to ensure that autistic children's and young people's self-esteem holds up when challenged by people who do not understand them or their autism. Parents play a vital role in teaching their autistic children and teens self-advocacy skills. Self-advocacy is the ability to say what you need in order to be able to do something or to access a particular place or an activity. Here are some examples of self-advocacy by autistic children and teens:

- 'I need to wear my sunglasses in class, because the lights in the hall hurt my eyes.'

- 'I need to spend time by myself to recharge my "social batteries".'

- 'I am autistic. This means I might see things differently to you, but that is okay. We all have the same rights.'

- 'I get agitated by the sun, so if it is hot I need to spend lunchtime in a cooler area.'

Aged 11–15 years

Signs that autistic children aged 11–15 years have some self-esteem include:

- They talk about themselves in a positive way, some or most of the time.

- Your child's friends treat your child and themselves with respect.

- They demonstrate love or affection for you and for other family members in their own way.

- Your child or teen is able to decline requests from peers to engage in negative or destructive activities.

- Discussions around activities, pets and friends are largely positive.

- Your child does not frequently describe themselves in negative terms.

- Passionate interests are mostly focused on positive interests.

Aged 16–20 years

Signs that young people aged 16–20 years have some self-esteem include:

- Your child talks and acts in a way that shows they have a mostly or increasingly positive self-view.

- Your child's friends treat your child and themselves with respect.

- If asked or encouraged by peers to engage in negative or destructive activities (such as criminal acts, self-harm, or using illicit drugs), your child declines the offer.

- Your child understands that they have the right to decide who does what with their body.

- Your child demonstrates that they are comfortable or happy with being autistic.

- Your child is interested in and focused on future activities, such as further study or work.

- Your child demonstrates an ability, or an increasing ability, to speak up on their own behalf, in whatever way they are able to, against hostility or unjust criticism.

PROTECTIVE FACTORS FOR SELF-ESTEEM

Protective factors for self-esteem are similar to those for resilience. The basis of self-esteem and resilience is the place of safety. A family that supports the child as they develop and loves and respects them as they are is absolutely crucial. A 'family' does not need to be made up of any one configuration: it might include one parent, two parents or an extended group, and be composed of any combination of genders; it can be a birth family, a blended family, or a foster or adoptive family. If the family creates a place of safety for the child, then developing resilience, independence, self-esteem and self-worth will be that much easier, and so will learning to fail successfully.

As mentioned before, being able to self-advocate can also support self-esteem. Accepting who you are and understanding your strengths and support needs is key to self-advocacy. That understanding of an autistic child's or young person's strengths can help to counter the negative messages they may hear in the wider world, and indeed help them to be resilient and strong in their responses to those messages.

USEFUL RESOURCES FOR PARENTS OF AUTISTIC PRETEENS, TEENS AND YOUNG ADULTS

WEB-BASED RESOURCES

Autism Helpline (UK)
Tel: 0845 070 4004 (open Monday–Friday, 10.00am–4.00pm)
Email: autismhelpline@nas.org.uk

Autism Self-Advocacy Network
http://autisticadvocacy.org

Autism Self-Advocacy Network Australia and New Zealand
http://www.asan-au.org

Autism Spectrum Australia (Aspect)
(Autism non-government organisation and service provider)
www.autismspectrum.org.au

Carol Gray – Social Stories™
http://carolgraysocialstories.com/social-stories

Interoception resources
Interoception 101
http://web.seru.sa.edu.au/pdfs/Introception.pdf
(Specific activities to develop your child's connection to themselves and others)
https://mindfulbodyawareness.com/resources

Jessica Kingsley Publishers
(Books and resources around parenting autistic children and related topics)
www.jkp.com

Positively Autistic
(Autism information and advocacy group promoting understanding around autism in the media and through social media and radio programmes)
http://positivelyautistic.weebly.com

Resources at Hand
(Australian-based retailer of autism books and sensory and fidget toys)
www.resourcesathand.com.au/shop/index.php

SEN Assist
(Online resources for parents and teachers of autistic kids)
www.senassist.com/about.html

Sensory Processing Disorder Australia
www.spdaustralia.com.au/about-sensory-processing-disorder

Sleep Health
www.sleephealth.com.au

US Asperger and Autism Association
www.usautism.org

Yellow Ladybugs
(Australian-based advocacy and social group for girls on the autism spectrum and
their parents)
http://yellowladybugs.com.au

BOOKS

Aitken, K.J. (2014) *Sleep Well on the Autism Spectrum*. London: Jessica Kingsley Publishers.

Boyd, B. (2013) *Parenting a Teen or Young Adult with Asperger Syndrome (Autism Spectrum Disorder): 325 Ideas, Insights, Tips and Strategies*. London: Jessica Kingsley Publishers.

Goodall, E. (2013) *Understanding and Facilitating the Achievement of Autistic Potential*. Create Space Independent Publishing Platform.

Goodall, E. (2016) *The Autism Spectrum Guide to Sexuality and Relationships: Understand Yourself and Make Choices that are Right for You*. London: Jessica Kingsley Publishers.

Grandin, T. and Moore, D. (2016) *The Loving Push*. Arlington, TX: Future Horizons.

Groden, J., Kantor, A., Woodard, C.R. and Lipsitt, L.P. (2011) *How Everyone on the Autism Spectrum, Young and Old, Can…Become Resilient, Be More Optimistic, Enjoy Humor, Be Kind, and Increase Self-Efficacy: A Positive Psychology Approach*. London: Jessica Kingsley Publishers.

Heydt, S. (2016) *A Parents' ABC of the Autism Spectrum*. London: Jessica Kingsley Publishers.

Jackson, L. (2016) *Sex, Drugs and Asperger's Syndrome (ASD): A User Guide to Adulthood*. Foreword by Tony Attwood. London: Jessica Kingsley Publishers.

Nichols, S. with Moravcik, G.M. and Pulver Tetenbaum, S. (2009) *Girls Growing Up on the Autism Spectrum.* London: Jessica Kingsley Publishers.

Purkis, J., Goodall, E. and Nugent, J. (2016) *The Guide to Good Mental Health on the Autism Spectrum.* London: Jessica Kingsley Publishers.

BOOKS FOR AUTISTIC PRETEENS AND TEENS

Brukner, L. (2014) *The Kids' Guide to Staying Awesome and In Control: Simple Stuff to Help Children Regulate their Emotions and Senses.* London: Jessica Kingsley Publishers.

Hoopmann, K. and Kiss, J.S. (2015) *Elemental Island.* London: Jessica Kingsley Publishers.

Jackson, L. (2002) *Freaks, Geeks and Asperger Syndrome: A User Guide to Adolescence.* London: Jessica Kingsley Publishers.

The Students of Limpsfield Grange School and Vicky Martin (2015) *M is for Autism.* London: Jessica Kingsley Publishers.

Reynolds, K.E. (2015) *What's Happening to Ellie? A Book about Puberty for Girls and Young Women with Autism and Related Conditions.* London: Jessica Kingsley Publishers.

Musgrave, F. (2017) *The Asperger Teen's Toolkit.* London: Jessica Kingsley Publishers.

Reynolds, K.E. (2014) *Things Tom Likes: A Book about Sexuality and Masturbation for Boys and Young Men with Autism and Related Conditions.* London: Jessica Kingsley Publishers.

Reynolds, K.E. (2015) *What's Happening to Tom? A Book about Puberty for Boys and Young Men with Autism and Related Conditions.* London: Jessica Kingsley Publishers.

OTHER RESOURCES

Asperger's Parents Connect – Facebook page:
www.facebook.com/AspergersParentConnect

Autism and Resilience. Are You Sure? – Blog post
https://jeanettepurkis.wordpress.com/2014/09/21/autism-and-resilience-are-you-sure

Paula Sanchez – Looking Back and Thinking Forward
https://autisticmotherland.com

'Disability Resilience and Achieving the Supposedly Impossible' – Presentation for TEDx Canberra by Jeanette Purkis
www.youtube.com/watch?v=pqdGb4TraFk

Interview by autistic author and advocate Carly Fleischmann and actor Channing Tatum
www.youtube.com/watch?v=a34qMg0aF6w

Teaching Resilience to Children with Asperger Profiles – published on the Asperger/Autism Network site
www.aane.org/teaching-resilience-children-asperger-profiles

The Autism Show – Episode 14: 'Resilience and Independence for Young People on the Autism Spectrum'
http://autismshow.org/jeanette

AUTISM IN POPULAR CULTURE
Positive books about living with autism
Attwood, T., Evans, C.R. and Lesko, A. (2014) *Been There, Done That, Try This!* London: Jessica Kingsley Publishers.
Kim, C. (2014) *Nerdy, Shy and Socially Inappropriate*. London: Jessica Kingsley Publishers.
Lawson, W. (2000) *Life Behind Glass*. London: Jessica Kingsley Publishers.
Regan, T. (2014) *Shorts*. London: Jessica Kingsley Publishers.
Santomauro, J. (2012) *Autism All-Stars*. London: Jessica Kingsley Publishers.

Documentaries, films, and novels
Documentary: *Alone in a Crowded Room*, directed by Lucy Paplinska, 2010.

Film: *Adam*, directed by Max Meyer, 2009.

Film: *Extremely Loud & Incredibly Close*, directed by Stephen Daldry, 2011.

Film: *Mozart and the Whale*, directed by Petter Naess, 2005.

Film: *My Name Is Khan*, directed by Karan Johar, 2010.

Film: *Temple Grandin*, directed by Mick Jackson, 2010.

Novel: *The Curious Incident of the Dog in the Night-Time*, Mark Haddon. London: Vintage, 2004.

Novel: *The Rosie Project*, Graeme Simsion. London: Simon and Schuster, 2014.